Cambridge English

Compact
Key for Schools

Teacher's Book

Emma Heyderman

CAMBRIDGE
UNIVERSITY PRESS

University Printing House, Cambridge CB2 8BS, United Kingdom

One Liberty Plaza, 20th Floor, New York, NY 10006, USA

477 Williamstown Road, Port Melbourne, VIC 3207, Australia

314–321, 3rd Floor, Plot 3, Splendor Forum, Jasola District Centre, New Delhi – 110025, India

79 Anson Road, #06–04/06, Singapore 079906

Cambridge University Press is part of the University of Cambridge.

It furthers the University's mission by disseminating knowledge in the pursuit of
education, learning and research at the highest international levels of excellence.

www.cambridge.org
Information on this title: www.cambridge.org/9781107618725

© Cambridge University Press 2014

First published 2014

20 19 18 17 16 15 14 13 12 11 10 9 8 7 6 5 4

Printed in Great Britain by CPI Group (UK) Ltd, Croydon CR0 4YY

A catalogue record for this publication is available from the British Library

ISBN 978-1-107-61863-3 Student's Book without answers with CD-ROM
ISBN 978-1-107-61880-0 Workbook without answers with Audio CD
ISBN 978-1-107-61872-5 Teacher's Book
ISBN 978-1-107-61868-8 Class Audio CD
ISBN 978-1-107-61874-9 Presentation Plus
ISBN 978-1-107-61879-4 Student's Pack (Student's Book without answers with CD-ROM, Workbook
without answers with Audio CD)

Additional resources for this publication at www.cambridge.org/compactkeyforschools

Contents

Map of the units

Unit	Topics	Grammar	Vocabulary	Functions
1 My family, my friends & me	People Daily life	*have got* Present simple Question words	Family Daily activities Describing people	Talking about routines and habits Asking for and telling the time Describing everyday activities
2 In my free time	Hobbies & leisure Personal opinions	Adverbs of frequency *Do you like …? / Would you like …?*	Free-time activities	Expressing preferences, likes and dislikes Giving and responding to invitations
3 Eating in, eating out	House & home Food & drink	*There is / are, a / an, some & any* *How much / many? a lot, a little, a few* *(don't) have to*	House & furniture Food & drink	Saying where things are Describing food Ordering food Expressing obligation
4 What are you doing now?	Sport Clothes	Present continuous Present simple vs present continuous	Sport Clothes	Talking about what people are doing now Describing what people are wearing
5 Great places to visit	Places & buildings Shopping	Past simple *ago* Time expressions *in / at / on*	Places Days & dates	Describing places Talking about dates Talking about events in the past
6 Getting there	Transport Travel	Comparative adjectives Superlative adjectives	Transport Directions	Making comparisons Asking for and giving directions
7 School rules!	School & study Entertainment	*must / mustn't* *should / shouldn't* *can / could* Adverbs of manner	Education Musical instruments	Expressing rules and obligation Giving advice Talking about ability in the present and past
8 We had a great time!	Holidays Personal experiences	Past continuous Past simple & past continuous	Holiday activities Adjectives of opinion	Talking about events in progress in the past Giving opinions
9 What's on?	Entertainment & media Television	*be going to* Infinitives & *-ing* forms	Going out TV programmes Word-building	Making suggestions Talking about future plans
10 Are you an outdoors person?	The natural world Weather	*will, won't & may* First conditional	The countryside Weather & seasons	Following instructions Making predictions about the future Expressing certainty and doubt
11 Healthy body, healthy mind	Health & medicine Personal feelings	Present perfect *just* *yet / already* Present perfect with *for & since*	The body Health & illness Adjectives	Talking about recent past events Talking about health problems Discussing personal feelings
12 Technology & me	Communication Appliances	The passive: present The passive: past	Communication & technology Describing objects	Describing simple objects Checking understanding

Reading	Writing	Listening	Speaking
Part 2: Sentences about a family	Part 6: Descriptions of things people use every day	Part 3: A conversation about a school day	Part 1: Describing people
Part 3a: Five conversations	Part 7: Completing an email about a boy's family, friends and hobbies	Part 4: A conversation about a cinema club	Part 1: Asking and answering about free time
Part 5: An article about a boy from Mali	Part 8: Completing notes about a class dinner	Part 5: A talk about a school trip to a cookery school	Part 2: Asking and answering about a café and a museum
Part 4: An article about a young businessman	Part 9: An email about clothes	Part 1: Five short conversations	Part 2: Asking and answering about a sports shop and a magazine
Part 2: Sentences about a school trip to a football museum	Part 9: An email about a shopping trip	Part 5: Information about a Hollywood tour	Part 1: Questions about things you did this week
Part 3b: A telephone conversation about a party	Part 7: An email about a trip to San Francisco	Part 2: A conversation about getting to a birthday party	Part 2: Asking and answering about a boat tour and a transport museum
Part 1: Notices	Part 9: An email about school	Part 5: A talk by a new teacher	Part 1: Questions about school subjects
Part 4: An article about a holiday in Guadeloupe	Part 8: Completing notes about a teacher's wedding present	Part 2: A conversation about where friends stayed on holiday	Part 2: Asking and answering about a holiday and a travel programme
Part 3b: A telephone conversation about plans for the weekend	Part 9: A message to a friend about a show	Part 4: A conversation about an audition for a TV show	Part 1: Questions about plans for the evening and a holiday
Part 1: Notices	Part 8: Completing a booking form for a weekend trip	Part 1: Five short conversations	Part 2: Asking and answering about a camping trip and an adventure park
Part 5: An article about the history of glasses Part 3a: Five conversations	Part 6: Descriptions of words about health	Part 3: A conversation about a healthy living day	Part 1: Questions about yourself and the weekend
Part 4: An article about young people and technology	Part 7: Completing emails about a lost MP3 player	Part 2: A conversation about favourite things	Part 2: Asking and answering about a web page and a computer game

1 My family, my friends & me

Unit objectives

KEY FOR SCHOOLS TOPICS	people, daily life
GRAMMAR	*have got*, present simple, question words
VOCABULARY	family, time, daily activities, describing people
READING	Part 2: Choosing the correct word
WRITING	Part 6: *this* and *these* – singular and plural nouns
LISTENING	Part 3: Choosing the correct time
SPEAKING	Part 1: Answering the *Tell me about* ... question

People

Grammar

Grammar – *have got*

1 With books closed, write the question *Have you got an unusual family?* on the board. Invite a brief class discussion on what an unusual family might be, e.g. a lot of brothers and sisters, family members with the same names or birthdays, etc. Students open their books and do the exercise. Point out the small glossary under the text and make sure students understand the word *twin*.

> **Answers**
>
> 1 False (I've got a twin brother and we've got two sisters.)
> 2 True (I've got the same name as my dad and his dad.)
> 3 True (I've got the same birthday as my sister, my mum and her sister.)

2 Encourage the students to tell you when we use *have got* (with *I*, *you*, *we*, *they*) and *has got* (with *he*, *she*, *it*).

> **Answers**
>
> Words to underline:
> Title: Have you got
> Jack: Yes! I've got
> Roz: Yes, we have.; I've got the same
> Greg: I've got a twin; we've got two sisters.
>
> 1 We use *have* or *has* and *not*
> 2 We use *Have I/you/we/they got ...?* or *Has he/she/it got...?*

3 Point out that all the examples of mistakes in the 'correct the mistake' exercises in this book are taken from real Key or Key for School exam scripts. Refer students to the Grammar reference on page 78. They can use these pages before or during the exercises. They can also use them to help them revise.

> **Answers**
>
> 2 My dad ~~is~~ = has got   3 This city ~~have~~ got = has got   4 It's a big swimming pool = It's got a   5 My phone ~~isn't~~ got = hasn't got   6 we ~~are~~ a lot of food = we've got

4 Encourage the students to read the whole text first before they start writing. Check they understand *nickname*.

> **Answers**
>
> 2 Have ... got   3 haven't (have not) got   4 've (have) got
> 5 's (has) got   6 hasn't (has not) got   7 've (have) got   8 have got

Further practice

In pairs, students ask and answer questions about their names and their family and friends' names. Brainstorm a list of possible question on to the board first, e.g. *Have you got an unusual name? Have your friends got nicknames? Has your brother got an unusual name?*

> See the Workbook and CD ROM for further practice.

Reading

Part 2

Vocabulary – Family

1 With books closed, brainstorm a list of family words and write them on the board. Make sure the list includes the words needed in this exercise. Encourage the students to find male and female pairs of words, e.g. brother & sister, son & daughter, etc.

With books open, ask the students to look at Roz's family tree first. Ask and answer questions around the class about it, e.g. *Has Roz got any brothers or sisters? What are Roz´s parents' names? Has she got any cousins?*, etc. Encourage the students to read Roz's email first before they complete it. With a weaker class, read the email through first with the answers before they start writing.

Further practice

The students could draw their own family tree and then tell their partner about their family.

> **Answers**
>
> 2 parents   3 aunt   4 uncle   5 children   6 cousins
> 7 grandfather   8 wife   9 sons

2 In this exercise, ask students to work in pairs and think about where they might say these sentences in order to help them. They can share their ideas with the class when you check the answers.

> **Answers**
>
> 2 ✓   3 ✓   4 ✓   5 ✓

3 Read the Exam tip as a class. Point out that these sentences are similar to those in Exercise 2 but here there is more information before and after each word which the students need to read. They can now choose the correct answer because of that.

> **Answers**
>
> 2 hair   3 begins   4 kinds   5 sure

Exam task

Ask the students to read the instructions for the Exam task and to tell you what they have to do in this part. Point out that the first sentence in the exam instructions will tell them what the sentences are about, i.e. Meg's family. Encourage the students to read the complete sentence first and try to think of a possible answer before they look at the three answers and choose the correct one.

> **Answers**
>
> 1 B   2 B   3 C   4 A   5 B

Writing

Part 6

1 With books closed, write *In my school bag, I've got ...* on the board. Go around the class asking each student to tell you at least one possible object, e.g. *a book, a pencil case*, etc. Ask the students to open their books, read the short text and identify the objects in the pictures before they write. In pairs they ask and answer questions with *Have you got ...?* about their school bags, e.g. *Have you got an old toy in your school bag? Yes, I have. What about you?*

> **Answers**
>
> 1 toy   2 diary   3 comb   4 pens, pencils   5 snack

2 Encourage the students to look at the Exam task and to tell you what they have to do in this part. Remind them that the first sentence of the instructions will tell them what the sentences are about; i.e. everyday objects. Read through the Exam tip as a class and ask the students which of the answers will be singular nouns and which will be plural.

> **Suggested answers**
>
> 2 purse, wallet   3 pen, pencil   4 trainers, football boots
> 5 violin, guitar   6 mobile, computer

3 Ask the students to look at the Exam task again. Point out that we know how many letters there are in each word, because the first letter is there and then there is one space for each other letter in the word. Ask the students to count the number of spaces for each word in this exercise so that they know how many letters there are in each word.

> **Answers**
>
> 2 purse   3 pen   4 trainers   5 violin   6 mobile

Exam task

Encourage the students to read the sentences and think of possible words before they look at the first letter and spaces. Remind them to look out for words like *this* or *these* which will tell them if the word is singular or plural. Also remind them to count the number of spaces.

> **Answers**
>
> 1 umbrella   2 bag   3 diary   4 watch   5 chairs

4 Do two or three examples first as a class using the sample answers below.

> **Suggested answers**
>
> 1 I put my pens and pencils in this. (pencil case)   2 I sleep in this at night. (bed)   3 I do my homework on this. (desk)   4 I brush my teeth with this (toothbrush).   5 I write my school work in this. (notebook).

Daily life

Grammar & vocabulary

Vocabulary – Daily activities

1 If necessary, revise the time in English by writing several examples on the board and asking students *What's the time?* Point out that they might hear different ways of asking the question (*What's the time?* or *What time is it?*) and telling the time (*It's seven forty* or *It's twenty to eight.*)

Do the first time as a class, then ask students to work in pairs asking and answering the question.

> **Answers**
>
> 1 What's the time in 1? It's seven forty or twenty to eight.
> 2 What's the time in 2? It's nine thirty or half past nine.
> 3 What's the time in 3? It's twelve fifty-five or five to one.
> 4 What's the time in 4? It's three fifteen or a quarter past three.
> 5 What's the time in 5? It's ten forty-five or a quarter to eleven.
> 6 What's the time in 6? It's eleven thirty-five or twenty-five to twelve.

2 Students look at Lee's photo album first to try to identify the verbs before they read the expressions 1–8.

> **Answers**
>
> 2 G   3 F   4 E   5 C   6 B   7 A   8 H

3 ◯━━1 Before the students listen, they should try to predict what time Lee does the things in the photos, e.g. *I think Lee walks to school at 8.30. What about you?*

> **Answers**
>
> 2 8.45   3 9.00   4 1.20 / 13.20   5 4.00 / 16.00   6 4.10 / 16.10   7 8.00 / 20.00   8 9.30 / 21.30

> **Recording script**
>
> Friend: Tell me about what you do every day, Lee.
> Lee: Well,(1) I usually wake up at 8 o'clock. I have a shower and I have breakfast. I leave home at a quarter to nine and I walk to school with my friends. (3) School starts at nine o'clock and if we're late, the teacher gets angry.
> Friend: Really? Do you have lunch at school?
> Lee: Yes, I do. (4) We have lunch at twenty past one.
> Friend: What do you do after school?
> Lee: School finishes at three forty-five and (5) I get home at four o'clock. I usually have a snack like a piece of bread or some biscuits and then (6) I do my homework at about ten past four. We have dinner

when my parents get home and then (7) at eight
o'clock, we all watch TV together.

Friend: What time do you go to bed?

Lee: My sister goes to bed at nine o'clock and (8) I go to
bed at half past nine.

Grammar – Present simple

4 With books closed, ask the students questions about the
present simple using the rules, e.g. *When do we add –s or
–es to the verb? How do we make the negative, questions
and short answers?* If necessary, refer the student to the
Grammar reference on page 78.

Answers

1 c 2 a 3 b

5 Remind the students that there is only one mistake in each
of these sentences.

Answers

2 don't = doesn't 3 watch = watches 4 Do = Does
5 cost = costs 6 start the match? = does the match start?
7 doesnt = doesn't 8 I'm not = I don't

6 Do the first two sentences as a class. Point out that the times
are probably not true for the students so that they will need
to write a sentence in both the negative and the affirmative,
giving the correct information.

Suggested answers

2 I don't walk to school with my friends at 8.30. I catch the bus
at 8.10.
3 School doesn't start at 9.00. It starts at 8.30.
4 I don't have lunch at 12.00. I have lunch at 1.00.
5 My friends don't do their homework at 4.00. They do their
homework at 5.30.
6 My mum doesn't get home at 6.00 She gets home at 7.00.
7 We don't watch TV at 7.00. We watch TV at 8.30.
8 My best friend goes to bed at 10.00. He doesn't go to bed at
8.30.

See the Workbook and CD ROM for further practice
on Grammar & Vocabulary.

Listening

Part 3

1 [2] Ask the students to read the instructions in the
Exam task and to tell you what they have to do in this part:
listen to Scott talking about his school day and choose
the correct answer. Encourage the students to look at the
picture and to say what is unusual about Scott's day. Read
the Exam tip as a class. Ask the students to work in pairs
and take turns to read and say the times.

Answers

1 a 2 a 3 a

Recording script

Amanda: Hi, Scott! How are you?

Scott: Oh hi, Amanda! I'm tired!

Amanda: Well, don't go to bed so late!

Scott: But I don't. I watch sports on TV and (1) then I go to
bed at about nine fifteen. The problem is I wake up
really early.

Amanda: Why's that?

Scott: I take the boat to school now, and it goes at half past
seven in the morning so (2) my mum wakes us up at
a quarter past six. We have breakfast and (3) leave
home at seven.

Exam task

[3] Encourage the students to read through all the
questions before they listen and to ask you for help with
any words they don't understand. Point out that in the exam
they will listen to each recording twice. Play the recording
once. Students can help each other with any answers
they didn't hear. Play the recording again. If you wish,
photocopy the recording script on page 94 for each student.
Ask them to underline the sentences which give them the
answers. Play the recording again.

Answers

1 C 2 B 3 A 4 A 5 B

Recording script

Listen to Scott talking to his cousin Amanda about his school day.
For each question, choose the right answer (A, B or C).

Amanda: Hi, Scott! How are you?

Scott: Oh hi, Amanda! I'm tired!

Amanda: Well, don't go to bed so late!

Scott: But I don't. I watch sports on TV and then I go to bed
at about nine fifteen. (0) The problem is I wake up
really early.

Amanda: Why's that?

Scott: I take the boat to school now, and (1) it goes at half
past seven in the morning, so my mum wakes us up
at a quarter past six. We have breakfast and leave
home at seven.

Amanda: So have you changed schools, then?

Scott: Yes. The school on our island is for six to eleven year
olds. (2) Now I'm twelve, I go to school on another
island with my sister Tanya. She's fourteen now.

Amanda: Oh, I see. So do you get home late in the evening?

Scott: Quite late. The boat back home is two hours after
school. (3) My mum's sister lives near the school so
we go and have dinner at her house.

Amanda: When do you have time to do your homework?

Scott: (4) We usually find a quiet table on the boat. When
we get home, we watch TV, listen to music or use the
computer.

Amanda: And what's your new school like?

Scott: Great! (5) I like my maths teacher best but the English
and sports classes are cool, too!

Amanda: Sounds good! When can I come and visit?

CLIL Geography: In small groups, students choose four or five islands around Great Britain and research each one. They find out about the population and services, e.g. schools and shops. Students produce a short report on each of their chosen islands. As a class, they produce a large map of Great Britain and stick their reports near their chosen islands.

Grammar – Question words

2 With books closed, brainstorm some questions and write them on the board. Encourage the students to tell you when we use each one. If necessary, help the students by asking questions, e.g. *What word do we use to ask about a place?* (Where) *A time?* (What time or When) *A date?* (When?), etc.

> **Answers**
> 2 Where 3 What time 4 How 5 When 6 What

3 Check the students' answers and then encourage the students to ask and answer the questions in pairs. Alternatively, divide the class into two or three teams and invite one student to come to the front to be the quizmaster. All the other students close their books. The quizmaster asks the questions and the teams have to answer them correctly in full sentences.

> **Answers**
> 1 a 2 a 3 a 4 b 5 b 6 a

4 Explain that to write the questions students have to choose one word or phrase from each box. As a class, make two or three questions together. If necessary, remind the students how to form present simple questions and that we use *do* with *I, you, we, they* and *does* with *he, she, it*. In pairs, students take turns to ask and answer their questions.

> **Suggested answers**
> Where do you go to school? What time does your brother wake up? When does your mum go to work? How do you go to school? Where do your friends do their homework?

Speaking

Part 1

Vocabulary – Describing people

1 Revise vocabulary to describe people (e.g. *curly / straight, long / short, dark / fair* + *hair; tall / short; brown / green / blue eyes*, etc.). With a stronger class, encourage the students to describe the people before they read the sentences.

Further practice
Students write descriptions of people they know; e.g. their teacher, best friend, etc.

> **Answers**
> 2 A 3 D 4 C

2 Begin by giving the class an example. Describe someone in the room, perhaps yourself, and encourage the students to say who it is. Check students' work as they write their sentences in pairs.

3 Students work in groups of six so each group has to listen to three descriptions. They follow the example and use the question and answer *Is it ...? Yes, it is / No, it isn't.* Fast finishers continue to describe more people they know.

4 🔘 **4** Point out that there are two parts to the Speaking Exam. In Part 1, the examiner will ask each candidate some personal questions. At the end of Part 1, the examiner will ask a *Tell me about ...* question.

> **Answers**
> 1 your English teacher 2 your school day

> **Recording script**
>
> Examiner: Ana, tell me about (1) your English teacher.
> Ana: Mrs Reed.
> Examiner: Jon, tell me about (2) your school day.
> Jon: Well, I wake up at a quarter past eight. I walk to school with my friends. School starts at nine o'clock. After school, I do my homework and then I watch TV.

5 Read the Exam tip as a class. Remind students they need to speak in full sentences of at least 4 or 5 words.

> **Answers**
> Jon gives the best answer because he speaks in full sentences and he says more than Ana.

6 Elicit from the class that Ana doesn't give a good answer because 'Mrs Reed' isn't a full sentence and Ana doesn't answer with at least three sentences.

> **Suggested answers**
> 2 She's got short, dark hair and blue eyes.
> 3 She goes to school by car.
> 4 She doesn't have lunch at school.
> 5 I like her because she's very nice.

Exam task

Students work in pairs. Give them time to prepare their answers before they do the task. Remind them to use full sentences and answer with at least three sentences.

> **Suggested answers**
> 1 A: Tell me about your school day.
>   B: I wake up at 7.30. I go to school with my dad. School starts at 8.30. After school, I walk home and then I do my homework.
> 2 A: Tell me about your favourite teacher.
>   B: Her name's Mrs Reed. She's got short, dark hair and blue eyes. She goes to school by car. She doesn't have lunch at school. I like her because she's very nice.
> 3 A: Tell me about what you do at the weekend.
>   B: I wake up at 9.00. I play football with my friends or we ride our bikes. On Sunday, I go to my grandparents' house.
> 4 A: Tell me about your best friend.
>   B: His name is Lucas. He's got short, dark hair and blue eyes. He's quite tall. I like him because he's very funny.

2 In my free time

Unit objectives

KEY FOR SCHOOLS TOPICS	hobbies & leisure, personal opinions
GRAMMAR	adverbs of frequency, *Do you like ...?/ Would you like ...?*
VOCABULARY	free time activities, expressions of like and dislike
READING	Part 3a: Thinking of a possible answer
WRITING	Part 7: Using the correct pronoun
LISTENING	Part 4: Spelling names correctly
SPEAKING	Part 1: Answering questions about free time activities

Hobbies & leisure

Grammar & vocabulary

Vocabulary – Free-time activities

1 Explain that in many schools in the UK and USA, there are different school clubs which the students can join. Ask the students to look at the noticeboard and say which of the clubs look interesting. Students work in pairs.

Answers

2 B 3 D 4 G 5 F 6 E 7 H 8 A

2 Encourage the students to read the whole message first before they complete it. Point out that these are all examples of verb + noun combinations / collocations and it is a good idea to learn these words as chunks, rather than as separate words, e.g. *take photos* rather than *take* and *photos*.

Answers

2 watch 3 sleep 4 listen 5 play 6 draw

Grammar – Adverbs of frequency

3 Check that students know what an adverb of frequency is first. Point out that it might be a short word like *usually* or *sometimes* or it might be a longer expression like *once a month*. Refer students to the Grammar reference on page 79.

Answers

1 after 2 before 3 both answers correct

4 After they have completed the exercise, encourage the students to make a note of typical mistakes e.g. *one times = once*, we don't use a negative verb with *never* and we use *every* and not *all* with *day – I wake up early every day.*

Answers

2 The classes are ~~all~~ Monday and Wednesday = every
3 They ~~often are~~ = are often
4 They ~~some times~~ watch = sometimes
5 I ~~don't never~~ eat = never
6 ~~ussually~~ = usually
7 ~~two times~~ a month = twice
8 ~~Always she~~ cooks = She always cooks

5 Point out that the students need to read the complete sentence first before they choose the word.

Answers

2 never 3 three times a week 4 every day 5 always 6 once a year

CLIL Maths – using graphs: In small groups, the students design a class survey about free-time activities using *How often do you ...?* or *Do you ever ...?* This could be an oral survey or the students could use a free online survey tool like Survey Monkey to create a written survey. When the students have done their survey, they should present the results using bar graphs and pie charts.

See the Workbook and CD ROM for further practice on Grammar & Vocabulary.

Listening

Part 4

1 Point out that there are five parts to the Listening Paper and that the task in Parts 4 & 5 is similar, i.e. the students need to complete some notes with times, places, names, etc. In Part 4, they listen to two people whereas in Part 5, they listen to one person. Read through the Exam tip as a class.

Answers

1 two
2 1 a time 2 where the club is 3 name of a film 4 a price 5 an email address

2 If the students don't know anything about these famous people, read out the information below and see if the students can guess who it is, e.g.

Teacher: *His name is Johnny Depp. He was born in the USA on 9 June 1963. He plays Jack Sparrow.*, etc.

Student: *Is it photo 1?*

Suggested answers

1 Johnny Depp: Born in the USA, 9 June 1963. Plays Jack Sparrow in the *Pirates of the Caribbean*.
2 Dakota Fanning: Born in the USA, 23 February 1994. Has been in *The Twilight Saga*.
3 Taylor Lautner: Born in the USA, 11 February 1992. Has been in *The Twilight Saga*.
4 Jaden Smith: Son of Will Smith. Born in the USA, 8 July 1998. Has been in *The Karate Kid*.

3 5 If necessary, revise the alphabet and the sounds with the class. Encourage the students to group the letters into seven sound groups:

/ei/	/i:/	/e/	/ai/	/əu/	/u:/	/a:/
A,H,J,K	B,C,D,E,G,P,T,V	F,L,M,N,S,X,Z	I,Y	O	Q,U,W	R

Answers

2 Hannah Dakota Fanning   3 Taylor Daniel Lautner
4 Jaden Syre Smith

Recording script

Paula:	Hi, Sheila!
Sheila:	Oh hi, Paula! Can you help me with the spelling of the full names of these famous people?
Paula:	Sure! The first one's Johnny Depp. (1) <u>His full name is John J–O–H–N Christopher C–H–R–I–S–T–O–P–H–E–R Depp D–E–Double P.</u>
Sheila:	<u>And what about Dakota Fanning? How do you spell that?</u>
Paula:	<u>Well, her full name is Hannah Dakota Fanning.</u> (2) <u>That's H–A–Double N–A–H D–A–K–O–T–A F–A–Double N–I–N–G.</u>
Sheila:	Thanks! And this one is Taylor Lautner, I mean Taylor Daniel Lautner. How do you spell that?
Paula:	(3) <u>It's T–A–Y–L–O–R D–A–N–I–E–L L–A–U–T–N–E–R.</u>
Sheila:	Cool! And that's Jaden Syre Smith, isn't it?
Paula:	Yes, you're right. Do you want me to spell his name, too?
Sheila:	Yes, please!
Paula:	(4) <u>It's J–A–D–E–N S–Y–R–E S–M–I–T–H.</u>
Sheila:	Thanks, Paula.

Exam task

6 Encourage the students to read the Exam task and to tell you what it is about (a cinema club). Play the recording twice and make sure that the students spell the email address in question 5 correctly.

You can photocopy the recording script on page 94 for each student. They listen again and underline the sentences that give the answers.

Answers

1 5.15   2 computer room   3 New Moon   4 £3.80   5 jaykes

Recording script

You will hear a boy, Ben, asking a friend about a cinema club.
Listen and complete each question.

Ben:	Hello, Hannah.
Hannah:	Hi, Ben.
Ben:	Hannah, I'm thinking of joining the Cinema Club. You're a member, aren't you?
Hannah:	Yes, I am. It's brilliant!
Ben:	When do you meet?
Hannah:	We meet once a week, on Monday afternoons.
Ben:	What time?
Hannah:	Well, some of us have got hockey training from 4 to 5 p.m. (1) <u>so the club meets at 5.15 p.m., when everyone can come.</u>
Ben:	That sounds OK. Do you still meet in the library?
Hannah:	(2) <u>We've just moved to the computer room,</u> which is opposite the library. It's got a much better screen.

Ben:	Oh, yes. I know where it is. What do you do in the club?
Hannah:	Well, one of us usually chooses a film, we watch it and then we talk about it. Last week, we saw *Push* with Dakota Fanning. (3) <u>Next week, we're going to watch *New Moon*.</u> You know, the one with Taylor Lautner in it. You should come!
Ben:	How much does it cost?
Hannah:	It's £1.60 a week or (4) <u>£3.80 a month.</u>
Ben:	Cool! Who do I need to speak to?
Hannah:	Send an email to (5) <u>jaykes@cinemaclub.com</u> . That's <u>J–A–Y–K–E–S.</u>
Ben:	Great! I'll do that tonight.

4 **7** Point out that we say *at* for '@' and *dot* for '.'

Answers

jaykes at cinema club dot com

Recording script

Ben:	Cool! Who do I need to speak to?
Hannah:	Send an email to (1) <u>jaykes@cinema club.com</u> . That's J–A–Y–K–E–S.
Ben:	Great! I'll do that tonight.

5 Read the cinema club address together as an example.

Answers

What's the email address for the cinema club? It's maria@cinemaclub.com
What's your best friend's email address? It's john@bestmail.com
What's the email address for the school? It's petershighschool@highschool.com
What's your email address? It's ana@coolmail.com

Further practice

In small groups, students ask and answer questions about their school clubs and after-school activities.

Grammar

Grammar – *Do you like...? / Would you like...?*

1 In pairs, students read the dialogue together. Ask which question we use to ask someone if they like something (*Do you like + ...ing?*) and which question we use to invite someone to do something (*Would you like + infinitive?*).

Suggested answers

Sam likes eating food from all over the world but he doesn't want to join Ruby's club. He isn't interested in cooking.

2 Encourage the students to read the conversation with gaps all the way through first before they complete it. Refer students to the Grammar reference on page 79.

Answers

2 Do you like reading   3 Would you like to come   4 Would you like to go   5 Do you like playing   6 Would you like to watch

Further practice

In pairs, students take the part of A or B.

3 With books closed, invite different students to do things and ask for a response, e.g. *Would you like to go to the cinema? No. Would you like to play a game? Yes.* Point out that a short answer like *yes* and *no* sounds rude in English and brainstorm some longer replies, e.g. *Yes, please. No, thanks.* Write these on the board.

> **Answers**
>
> I'd love to , I'm afraid not..

4 If you wrote possible replies on the board in Exercise 3 (see above), encourage the students to compare their ideas with the expressions in the book.

> **Answers**
>
> Yes: I'd love to. Sure! Good idea.
> No: No, thanks! I'm afraid not. I'm sorry, I can't.

5 Check that the students understand the events by asking them which sound the most / least interesting. Model the first conversation in the example with a strong student. Encourage fast finishers to make up some more dialogues.

> **Suggested answers**
>
> A: Would you like to run a half marathon with me?
> B: I'm afraid not. I can't run fast.
> A: Would you like to go camping this weekend?
> B: I'm sorry, I can't. I'm busy this weekend.
> A: Would you like to visit the Science Museum with me tomorrow?
> B: Good idea! I love that museum.

> See the Workbook and CD ROM for further practice.

Reading

Part 3a

1 Students look at the Exam task and say what they have to do in this part. Explain that Reading Part 3 has two parts and the Exam task on this page focuses on the first part. Read the Exam tip as a class. Point out that although they should try to think of their own answer first, they will need to choose one of the given answers. After the students have done the exercise, write their suggested answers on the board.

> **Suggested answers**
>
> 2 Would you like to come with me?   3 No, I can't draw.
> 4 Really?   5 Yes, please! I love camping.

2 If you have written the students' suggestions on the board in Exercise 1, compare their ideas with these answers. Tell the students to cross out the answers as they use them.

> **Answers**
>
> 2 Can you sing?   3 Not often.   4 So do I.   5 I'm afraid not. I'm busy.

Exam task

Remind the students that they should try to think of a possible reply before they read the three answers.

> **Answers**
>
> 1 A   2 C   3 A   4 B   5 B

3 & 4 Do the example and, if necessary, question 1 together as a class. Say *Fine thanks* to the class and encourage the students to tell you a suitable question (*How are you?*). Do the same with *How do you do?* (*How do you do?*).

> **Suggested answers**
>
> 1 How often do you go to the cinema? B Sometimes, with my friends.
>   I think Johnny Depp is a great actor. C Do you think so?
> 2 There's a pencil on the floor. A Whose is it?
>   Don't write! B I haven't written anything.
> 3 What do you like doing in your free time? B Listening to music.
>   Have you got your keys? C I hope so.
> 4 Have you got your maths book? A I think so.
>   Can you close the window? C It isn't open.
> 5 Would you like to play tennis at the weekend? A I'm busy on Saturday.
>   Do you ever play tennis? C Not very often.

Personal opinions

Speaking

Part 1

1 Encourage the students to tell you which of the words have a stronger negative or positive meaning; i.e. *hate, be terrible at, be brilliant at, love*.

> **Answers**
>
> | Negative | Positive |
> | --- | --- |
> | hate | be good at |
> | don't like | enjoy |
> | be terrible at | prefer |
> | be bad at | love |
> | | like |
> | | be brilliant at |
> | | be interested in |

2 Point out that after all these expressions, we use the *–ing* form. Also point out that the students can use the activities in the box or their own ideas.

> **Suggested answers**
>
> 2 playing computer games, cooking   3 going to concerts, dancing
> 4 reading books, writing emails   5 trying new food, cooking

3 Remind the students that the question here is *Do you like + ing?* Encourage the students to answer with a variety of the opinion expressions.

> **Suggested answers**
>
> Do you like playing computer games? Yes, I do. I'm good at playing computer games.
> Do you like going to concerts? Yes, I do. I'm interested in going to concerts.
> Do you like reading books? Yes, I do. I enjoy reading books.
> Do you like writing emails? No, I don't. I hate writing emails.

4 Remind the students that in Part 1, the examiner will ask personal information questions, e.g. about their free-time activities. In pairs, students read and complete the dialogue, then write down the missing words. Don't check them yet.

5 🔘 **8** Play the recording for students to check their answers. Then ask students *Are the answers good or not?* (*They're not good because they are rather short*). Before reading the Exam tip, encourage the students to think of ways they could improve the answers.

Recording script

Examiner:	(1) What do you usually do at the weekend?
Candidate:	I listen to music.
Examiner:	(2) What other things do you do in your free time?
Candidate:	I watch TV.
Examiner:	(3) How often do you watch TV?
Candidate:	After dinner.

6 Elicit ideas from the class before they read the example.

Suggested answers

I watch TV with my family. We prefer watching films to watching sports.
I usually watch TV after dinner on weekdays. At weekends I sometimes watch TV in the morning.

Exam task

Point out that the examiner's third question will reflect the students' answer for question two, e.g.

2 What other things do you do? **I go swimming.**

3 How often do you **go swimming**? I go …

Remind Student B to use the opinion expressions (*I like, enjoy, prefer,* etc.) on this page and the adverbs of frequency. Encourage the students to take turns to be student A and B.

Suggested answers

A: What do you usually do at the weekend?
B: On Saturday morning, I usually do my homework. In the afternoon, I often meet my friends. I love watching films so I sometimes go to the cinema on Sunday afternoon.
A: What other things do you do in your free time?
B: I'm good at dancing so I go to dance classes.
A: How often do you go to dance classes?
B: I go to dance classes twice a week. We sometimes do a show on Saturday.

See the Workbook and CD ROM for further practice.

Writing

Part 7

1 Encourage the students to look at the Exam task and to say what they have to do in this part (complete an email). Point out to the students that if they write more than one word, the answer is not correct. Read the Exam tip as a class.

Answers

2 me 3 him 4 We 5 their 6 us 7 His 8 They

2 Elicit one or two sentences from the class first to check that everyone knows what to do. Either correct any mistakes with pronouns when the students make them or write a list of their mistakes on the board for them to correct when they have finished speaking.

Suggested answers

He's got a camera so he likes taking photos with it. I think he enjoys drawing because there's a picture. He plays the guitar because I can see one. I think his favourite football team is Barcelona because there's a poster and he loves watching films. I think his favourite film is *Star Wars*.

3 Encourage the students to read the email first without writing, pointing out that it is good exam technique to read through any text first to get a general idea. Ask some general questions to check that the students have understood the email, e.g. *Where is Kazuo from? Has he got any brothers or sisters? What is his best friend good at?*, etc.

Suggested answers

In his free time, Kaz likes listening to music and drawing pictures, he plays the guitar and he goes to the cinema. He sometimes has dinner in a pizza restaurant.

Exam task

Stress that they can write **one** word only. Students should check they have used the correct pronouns in 3, 5 and 9.

Answers

1 in 2 have 3 Their 4 at 5 me 6 to 7 play 8 a 9 we
10 about

Further practice

Students can use Kazuo's email to help them write their own message about themselves.

Sample answer

My name is Alejandre but my friends call me Alex. I'm 12 years old and I live in São Paulo, Brazil. I've got two brothers. Their names are Enzo and Vitor. My best friend Miguel is good at playing basketball and his favourite team is the Chicago Bulls. In my free time, I like watching films. On Saturdays, I always meet my friends and we go to the cinema. I also enjoy taking photos with my camera.

3 Eating in, eating out

Unit objectives

KEY FOR SCHOOLS TOPICS	house & home, food & drink
GRAMMAR	*There is / are, a / an, some & any, How much / many? a lot, a little, a few, (don't) have to*
VOCABULARY	house and furniture, food & drink
READING	Part 5: Choosing *some*, *any*, *few* or *little* correctly
WRITING	Part 8: Finding the correct information
LISTENING	Part 5: Writing down prices in pounds (£) correctly
SPEAKING	Part 2: Asking correct questions, answering questions about email addresses and websites

House & home

Grammar & vocabulary

Vocabulary – House & furniture

1 In pairs, ask the students to look at the pictures and to say what time of day it is and where the people are in each picture. (A bedroom; B living room; C kitchen; D Hall; E bathroom) Point out that Harun is a boy's name.

> **Answers**
> 2 C   3 B   4 A

2 Encourage the students to think of some more items to add to the table. Ask the students to find the items in the table in the pictures in Exercise 1.

> **Suggested answers**
>
> | bedroom | bathroom | living room | kitchen |
> |---|---|---|---|
> | desk, lamp, mirror | mirror, toilet, shower | bookshelf, sofa | cooker, cupboard, fridge, shelf, chair |

Grammar – *There is / are, a / an, some & any*

3 You could do this exercise as a memory test. Ask the students to look at the pictures for one or two minutes and then close their books. Read the sentences and elicit the answers. When the students have finished, ask them to underline examples of *There is* and *There are* and *a / an*, *some* and *any* and to say when we use each one. If necessary, refer the students to the Grammar reference on page 80.

> **Answers**
> 2 Angela   3 Harun   4 Noelia

4 Ask the students to say why the words are wrong, e.g. question 1: we usually use *some* in positive sentences and not *any*; question 2: we use *an* before a vowel sound, etc.

> **Answers**
> 2 a~~a~~ ice-cream = an   3 Behind my house ~~is there~~ = there is
> 4 don't bring ~~some~~ food = any   5 cooks ~~a~~ bread = some bread
> / bread   6 bring ~~a~~ tomatoes = some tomatoes   7 There ~~are~~ a
> lot of water = There is   8 ~~There's~~ = There are

Reading

Part 5

Grammar – *How much / many? a lot, a little, a few*

1 With books closed, ask the students if they know how to make an omelette and ask them for the ingredients. Students read the messages and check their ideas.

> **Answers**
> Students should underline: a lot of eggs, a little oil, a little salt, (a few potatoes)

2 Encourage the students to say which of the ingredients are countable and which are uncountable before they complete the rules. Refer students to the Grammar reference on page 80.

> **Answers**
> 1 countable   2 uncountable   3 & 4 countable and uncountable (in any order).

3 Encourage the students to read the whole text first and then to say if the nouns are countable or uncountable before they choose the correct words.

> **Answers**
> 1 much   2 little   3 many   4 few   5 little   6 many   7 little
> 8 much

Exam task

Encourage the students to read the instructions and to say what they have to do in this part: read a text and choose the best word. Read the Exam tip as a class. Ask the students to read the complete text first without writing. Then with books closed, they tell you what they learned about Mamadou. With books open, focus the students' attention on the first two spaces and ask them what words are missing. Remind them to look at the noun (beds) and to think about whether it is countable or uncountable, singular or plural.

> **Answers**
> 1 A   2 B   3 C   4 C   5 B   6 A   7 C   8 A

Further practice

In pairs, students ask and answer questions about what they have for breakfast and where they have it; e.g. *What do you have for breakfast? Where do you have it? Do you have it with your parents?*

CLIL Geography / Social Sciences: The information about Mamadou was taken from the Oxfam Cool Planet website which has information about kids from all over the world. Divide the class into three teams and give each team a food: pink carrots, cocoa or bananas. Each team looks at the website and finds some information about their food. They tell the rest of the class three facts. Give them some questions to help them, e.g. *Where do they grow these crops? Who buys them? How does this help the farmers?*

See the Workbook and CD ROM for further practice.

Food & drink

Grammar & vocabulary

Vocabulary – Food & drink

1 With books closed, brainstorm a list of food and drink onto the board. With books open, students try to find the words on the board in the pictures. Elicit other kinds of food and drink they can see. Tell them to read the complete descriptions and match them to the pictures with their pens down. They will complete the descriptions in Exercise 2.

Answers

2 Picture C   3 Picture A

2 Clear up any problems with vocabulary before the students start writing.

Answers

2 milk   3 fish   4 rice   5 onions   6 soup   7 chicken   8 juice

Further practice

In pairs, the students ask and answer questions about the food they like, e.g. *Do you like chicken, meat and fish? I like chicken and meat but I don't like fish very much.*

Grammar – *(don't) have to*

3 Point out that many schools in the UK, Australia, South Africa and New Zealand have a 'tuck shop' which sells food, drink and often stationery, too.

Answers

1 fast food like burgers and pizza   2 at school

4 Students read the interview again and underline the answers in the text. Point out that we use *(don't) have to* to talk about things which are and aren't necessary.

Answers

2 F (I have to pay for my lunch before school starts.)
3 F (Two students have to collect our food from the tuck shop)
4 F (We don't have to wash up.)

5 Check that the students know how to write the positive, negative and question form of *have to* first. If necessary, refer the students to the Grammar reference on page 80. Remind students to read the dialogue before writing.

Answers

2 Do you have to wake up   3 have to get up   4 Do you have to tidy   5 don't have to tidy   6 have to make   7 has to make 8 have to eat

Further practice

In pairs, students ask and answer questions about the things they have to do at home, e.g. *Do you have to wash up? Do you have to clean the floor? Do you have to tidy your room?*

See the Workbook and CD ROM for further practice on Grammar & Vocabulary.

Listening

Part 5

1 🔊 **9** Remind the students that Listening Part 5 is similar to Part 4 because the students have to complete notes, but in this part they listen to one person only. Ask the students to tell you what the listening is about (buying something in a fast food café). Read the Exam tip together. Tell students if they need to complete a price, this price will always be in pounds (£). Check they know how to write prices in pounds (£) and that we use a dot '.' to separate the pounds from the pence (£5.56). Point out that the answers are not in the same order on the recording so the students need to listen carefully. If necessary, play the recording several times.

Answers

2 £1.15   3 £2.80   4 £1.35   5 89p

Recording script	
Server:	Next customer, please!
Boy:	Oh, that's me!
Server:	Can I help you?
Boy:	Yes. Can I have a fried egg, please?
Server:	One or two eggs?
Boy:	One egg, please. How much is it?
Server:	(1) That's one pound seventy-five. Do you want bread and butter with that?
Boy:	Yes, please. No, wait. How much is an omelette?
Server:	That's two pounds twenty-seven or (3) two pounds eighty with cheese.
Boy:	OK. I'll have a cheese omelette and a slice of bread and butter, please.
Server:	Anything to drink?
Boy:	How much is a cup of hot chocolate?
Server:	(5) All our hot drinks are eighty-nine p. And how about a piece of cake too?
Boy:	Oh. OK. How much is it all?
Server:	So, a cheese omelette, (2) a slice of bread and butter for one pound fifteen, a cup of hot chocolate and (4) a piece of our special cake for one pound thirty five. That's six pounds nineteen.
Boy:	Here you are.
Server:	Enjoy your meal!

Further practice

In pairs, students ask and answer questions about the prices on the menu, e.g. *How much is the fried egg? It's £1.75.* Make sure that students know how to say the prices correctly before they begin.

2 Help the students if necessary by writing question prompts on the board, e.g. 1 How / get there? 2 What time / at school? 3 bring / anything special? 4 learn / to cook there?

> ### Suggested answers
> 1 How can we get there?   2 What time do we have to be at school?   3 Do we have to bring anything special?   4 Can we learn to cook there?

3 After students have read through the Exam task, ask them to say what information is missing in each space, e.g. 1 time, 2 place, 3 price, 4 item of stationery, 5 email address.

Exam task

🔘 10 Play the recording at least twice.

> ### Answers
> 1 7.45   2 dining room   3 £9.55   4 rubber   5 ellapetts

> ### Recording script
>
> *You will hear a teacher talking about a school trip to the Star Cookery School.*
>
> *Listen and complete each question.*
>
> Everyone shh! Please listen to me for a moment. I want to tell you about the school trip to the Cookery School on 16th February. (1) You have to be outside the school gates at seven forty-five because the bus leaves from there at 8 o'clock.
>
> There are some great things to see and do at the cookery school. We'll see how you can grow your own vegetables in the science room, we'll learn how to make pizza and chocolate cake in the kitchen, and then (2) we'll eat this food in the dining room.
>
> Now listen carefully! (3) You need to give me £9.55 before Thursday but please tell your parents that this includes the bus and £6.00 for lunch. You don't have to make sandwiches for this trip and you can't take any food into the cookery school anyway.
>
> Don't forget, (4) you'll need a pencil and a rubber but you don't have to bring a notebook. If your parents have any questions, they can phone me at the school or (5) they can email me at ellapetts@grantschool.com. Remember that's e–double l–a–p–e–double t–s. I think that's it for now.

Further practice

Ask students to tell you which of the questions in Exercise 2 they can now answer (all of the ones in the suggested answers).

4 Remind the students that they might be asked about the food they eat in Speaking Part 1. Encourage the students to answer in complete sentences. If necessary, model a good answer first.

> ### Suggested answers
> 1 I like chicken and chips. I also like eggs and omelettes.
> 2 I usually have lunch at my grandmother's house.
> 3 My mum and my dad cook in my house.
> Do you have to help? Yes, I do. I have to put the things on the table. I also have to clean the table when we finish.

Speaking

Part 2

1 Ask the students to look at the Exam task and to say what they have to do in this part. Point out that in Speaking Part 2, the candidates need to ask and answer questions about some information. They speak to each other and not the examiner. Each candidate takes turns to make complete questions using some questions prompts and to answer these questions using some information. Each candidate is given a different set of information and set of question prompts. Point out that the first word in each question in this exercise begins with a capital letter.

> ### Answers
> 2 What time does it open?   3 Are the snacks expensive?   4 Is there any hot food?   5 How much are the cold drinks?   6 How can I get more information?

2 Point out that the questions in this exercise and in the exam will not be in the same order as the information.

> ### Answers
> 2 e   3 b   4 c   5 d   6 f

3 🔘 11 Play the recording so that students can check their answers. Ask the students if the two exam candidates do this task well. (They do it well because the boy asks complete questions and the girl answers in complete sentences). There is more practice making questions, in the Speaking Section.

> ### Recording script
>
> | | |
> |---|---|
> | Male student: | (1) Where's the snack shop? |
> | Female student: | (a) It's opposite the library. |
> | Male student: | (2) What time does it open? |
> | Female student: | (e) It opens at break time. |
> | Male student: | (3) Are the snacks expensive? |
> | Female student: | (b) No, the snacks are cheap. |
> | Male student: | (4) Is there any hot food? |
> | Female student: | (c) Yes, there's soup. |
> | Male student: | (5) How much are the cold drinks? |
> | Female student: | (d) The cans are all 50p. |
> | Male student: | (6) How can I get more information? |
> | Female student: | (f) You can email jenny@snackshop.com. |

4 🔘 12 Read the Exam tip together as a class and ask the students if they remember how to say an email address in English. Then ask them to listen to how the addresses in the notices are said.

> ### Answers
> @ = at, www = double u double u double u, .com = dot com

> ### Recording script
>
> | | |
> |---|---|
> | Student: | Why don't you sell hot drinks like hot chocolate when it's cold? |
> | Jenny: | Good idea. Can you email your ideas to me? My email is jenny at snack shop dot com. And don't forget to visit my website. It's w-w-w dot snack shop dot com. |

5 Students work in pairs to ask and answer the questions. Elicit answers from different pairs.

> **Suggested answers**
>
> How can I get more information about the park café? You can send an email to pete@cafe.com
> Is there a website? Yes, it's www.cafe.com.

Further practice

In pairs, the students ask and answer questions about the websites they use and like, e.g. *What's your favourite website? It's www.youtube.com*

Exam task

Read the full exam instructions to the class before the students begin:

Student A, here is some information about a café in your town. Student B, you don't know anything about the café so ask Student A some questions about it. Now Student B, ask your questions about the café and Student A, you answer them.

World Food Café

Dishes from all over the world

Next to the museum

Main courses – only £10!

Monday – Saturday 11 a.m. – 3 p.m.

Visit: www.worldcafe.com

World Food Café

♦ where / café ?

♦ what kind / food ?

♦ time / open ?

♦ expensive ?

♦ website ?

Now Student B, here is some information about a Chocolate Museum in your town. Student A, you don't know anything about the museum so ask Student B some questions about it. Now Student A, ask your questions about the museum and Student B, you answer them.

Chocolate Museum

In the Chocolate Factory

Learn how to make chocolate!

Family ticket (2 adults and 3 children): £30

Tuesday – Sunday 10 a.m. – 5 p.m.

Visit: www.chocmuseum.com

Chocolate Museum

♦ where / museum ?

♦ what / do there ?

♦ open / every day ?

♦ cost ?

♦ more information ?

Check students are asking complete questions and that they are answering in complete sentences.

> **Suggested answers**
>
> **World Food Café**
> B: Where's the cafe?
> A: It's next to the museum.
> B: What kind of food can you eat there?
> A You can eat food from all over the world.
> B What time does it open?
> A: It opens at 11a.m.
> B: Is it expensive?
> A: No, main courses are only £10.
> B Is there a website?
> A: Yes, it's www.worldcafe.com
>
> **Chocolate Museum**
> A Where's the museum?
> B It's in the chocolate factory.
> A What can I do there?
> B You can learn how to make chocolate.
> A Is it open every day?
> B No, it's closed on Mondays.
> A: How much is it?
> B A family ticket is £30.
> A: How can I get more information?
> B: You can visit www.chocmuseum.com

Writing

Part 8

1 If possible, bring in some real life examples of notices, advertisements, emails and notices for the students to look at. Let them try to match the different types of notices to the ones in the book.

> **Answers**
>
> 2 a notice   3 an advertisement   4 some notes

2 In Writing Part 8, students will always need to read two different types of text and then complete some information.

> **Answers**
>
> 2 an email   3 some notes

3 Point out that it is good exam technique to look at the notes first and think about what sort of information is missing (and a possible answer). Read the Exam tip as a class.

> **Suggested answers**
>
> 2 Time to meet: 5 o'clock, 7.30 Imogen's Phone number: 897112, 456223, Travel by: bus, train Cost: £5, £7.50

Exam task

Remind the students that the answer could be in the advertisement or the email.

> **Answers**
>
> 1 Grey   2 6   3 564734   4 tram   5 4.75

Further practice

In pairs, the students ask and answer full questions about the class dinner, e.g. *Where is the dinner? It's at Dave's Pizzas. What time is it? It's at …*

What are you doing now?

Unit objectives

KEY FOR SCHOOLS TOPICS	sport, clothes
GRAMMAR	present continuous, present simple vs present continuous
VOCABULARY	sport, clothes
READING	Part 4: Underlining important words in the text
WRITING	Part 9: Answering all three questions, writing 25–35 words
LISTENING	Part 1: Underlining important words and looking at the three pictures
SPEAKING	Part 2: Asking correct complete questions

Sport

Grammar & vocabulary

Vocabulary – Sport

1 Give students five minutes working in small groups to write down as many different sports as they can. Explain what 'tips' (useful suggestions) are. Check answers.

> **Answers**
>
> ice hockey 4   fishing 2   swimming 6   table tennis 3
> basketball 5

Further practice

Create a table on the board with the class and encourage the students to keep a record of the new sports in the unit:

Sport	Equipment	Place
skateboarding ice hockey	skateboard hockey stick, helmet	skate park ice rink, etc.

2 Elicit from the class which sports are used with *play* (ball sports), *go* (... ing) and *do* (other sports). Encourage the students to add more sports to the table. Use the ones in Exercise 1 to begin with (go fishing / skateboarding / swimming; play basketball / table tennis / ice hockey). If you have created a Sports Table in Exercise 1 (see above), insert a *play / go / do* column before 'sport'.

> **Answers**
>
> play: football, golf
> go: cycling, skiing, ice-skating, surfing
> do: aerobics, athletics, martial arts

Further practice

In pairs, students ask and answer questions about the sports they do, e.g. *What sports do you do? How often do you do them? What are your favourite places to do sports?*

Grammar – Present continuous

3 Elicit the words that tell them the sport is tennis; i.e. *a racket*, *small yellow balls*, *hit a ball*, *win 40–15*. Students underline the examples of the present continuous in the text and say when we use it (an activity which is happening now) and how we form it (*be (not) + ... ing*).

4 Students try to correct the spelling mistakes. Then, they compare their corrections with the spelling rules of the *... ing* form in the Grammar reference on page 81.

> **Answers**
>
> 2 sitting   3 waiting   4 swimming   5 playing   6 listening

5 Remind students to read the dialogue before writing.

> **Answers**
>
> 2 'm (am) watching   3 Is the school team winning   4 is
> 5 's (is) playing   6 Is Ben sitting   7 isn't   8 's (is) buying
> 9 're (are) losing

> See the Workbook and CD ROM for further practice on Grammar & Vocabulary.

Listening

Part 1

1 Elicit what is different about this part of the listening paper, i.e. the students need to look at five sets of three pictures and answer a question about each set.

> **Answers**
>
> 1 five (plus an example)   2 one   3 three

2 Read the Exam tip as a class. Tell students to read the question carefully. Then look at the pictures and decide how each one answers the question. Underlining the important words and thinking about each picture will help them to focus on the correct information in the listening.

> **Answers**
>
> 1 What's Holly doing <u>now</u>?
> 2 A She's swimming B She's mountain biking C She's climbing

3 ⚪ 13 If necessary, play the recording twice. With a stronger class, encourage the students to say what question the other two pictures (A & B) answer.

> **Answer**
>
> C

> **Recording script**
>
> *Listen to Question 1 from the exam task.*
> *1 What's Holly doing now?*
> Boy: Holly wasn't at swimming practice today. Is she ill?
> Girl: No, she's fine. She's in the mountains with her family.
> Boy: Really? Is she mountain biking again?
> Girl: No, she's learning to climb. She's got a great teacher.

4 Remind the students that they will hear information about all three pictures but only one piece of information will answer the question on the exam paper correctly.

Answers

1 C   2 A   3 B

Exam task

14 Before they listen, encourage the students to read the questions and underline the important words. They should also look at the three pictures for each question and think about how the pictures answer each question, e.g.

2 How much is Jenny's new tennis racket?
A It's £35.; B It's £40.; C It's £45.

After they have completed the task, hand out photocopies of the recording script on page 95. Students underline the correct answer and circle the other items in the pictures that are mentioned.

Answers

2 B   3 C   4 A   5 B

Recording script

You will hear five short conversations.

You will hear each conversation twice.

There is one question for each conversation.

For each question, choose the right answer (A, B or C).

2 How much is Jenny's new tennis racket?

Boy: I love your new tennis shoes. Were they expensive?

Girl: No, they weren't. They were £35. My racket was more expensive.

Boy: Oh really? How much was that?

Girl: (2) I bought it online for £40. My sister paid £45 for hers.

3 What time does the hockey match start?

Girl: Excuse me. What time does the hockey match start?

Man: (3) It starts at half past four.

Girl: What time is it now? Am I late?

Man: No, it's only ten past four. Go for a walk and come back at twenty past four.

4 What is Simon drinking?

Girl: I'm thirsty after that race.

Simon: (4) This lemonade is really good. I bought it over there in the café.

Girl: Is there any juice?

Simon: I don't think so, but they've got hot chocolate if you prefer that.

5 Who is Maisie's table-tennis coach?

Maisie: That's my table-tennis coach over there.

Boy: Who? Is he that blond man over there with glasses?

Maisie: No, (5) he's got dark hair and he doesn't wear glasses.

Boy: Oh, I can see him now. He's standing over there next to Brendan.

Grammar & vocabulary

Vocabulary – Clothes

1 Pre-teach *wheelchair*. Encourage the students to answer in complete sentences e.g. *I think she plays basketball because …*

Answers

1 basketball   2 surfing   3 ice hockey

2 Read through the clothes as a class. Check that the students understand each word and can pronounce them correctly. Encourage the students to ask complete questions (*What's she wearing?*) and answer in full sentences (*She's wearing …*).

Suggested answers

1 She's wearing a basketball shirt, some shorts, some socks and some basketball shoes.
2 He's wearing shorts and a T-shirt.
3 She's wearing a shirt, some trousers, some boots and a helmet.

Grammar – Present simple vs present continuous

3 After matching the texts, in pairs students guess the meanings of some of the vocabulary from context; e.g. *teenage, competition, team, train, practice, match* and *medal*.

Answers

a 2   b 3   c 1

4 Check that students can identify the present simple and present continuous. Refer students to the Grammar reference on page 81.

Answers

PC: he's thinking about; she's getting ready; She's feeling excited
PS: comes, say, wants, trains, has to, plays, goes, hope

5 Ask students questions to see how much they know before they do this exercise, e.g. *Do we use the present simple or continuous to talk about the things we do every day? And the things which are happening now?*, etc. Also elicit the time adverbs we use with each one; e.g. *now, at the moment, today, this week* with the present continuous; *often, usually, every day, twice a week* with the present simple.

Answers

1 present simple   2 present continuous

6 Do this exercise in stages. First students read the whole text without writing. Then, they think about which verb goes in which space. Next they should look for words which tell them if it is the simple (*usually*) or continuous (*at the moment*). With a weaker class, first read the complete text to the class with the verbs in their correct form.

Answers

2 throws   3 trains   4 're (are) thinking   5 's (is) getting
6 wants

CLIL Sport: In small groups, students choose a country in another part of the world and find out information about a sport in that country which isn't normally played in the students' own country. Students should find information about the equipment needed, the clothes and the rules. The groups present their sport to the class using pictures and diagrams.

See the Workbook and CD ROM for further practice on Grammar & Vocabulary.

Reading

Part 4

1 Point out that this is the longest text in the Reading Paper. Give the students two or three minutes to complete the activity before checking answers as a class.

> **Answers**
>
> 1 an article   2 No, you have to say if seven sentences are right or wrong. If there is not enough information to answer 'Right' or 'Wrong', you have to choose 'Doesn't say'.

2 Point out that it is always a good idea to look at any titles, headings or photos first as these give an idea of what the text is about. Elicit ideas from the class.

> **Suggested answer**
>
> A boy who makes and sells sports shoes. He also does something good for other people.

3 Remind students that they should always read the whole text first to get a general idea before they look at the sentences and options. Give the students three minutes to read the article and answer the gist question.

> **Answer**
>
> When you buy a pair of Ben's sports shoes, he gives a free pair to somebody who needs them. They all look the same and they all cost $50.

4 Read the Exam tip with the class, reminding the students that they can write on the exam paper. Go over the example with the class, showing them that they would write 0 next to the sentence *Ben is an American teenager*. Ask them which words in the example sentence and the text match (from the USA – American). Ask them to individually do the same with sentence 1 and check the answer. The answer here is *Doesn't Say*. Point out that this means there is not enough information to say if the answer is right or wrong.

> **Answer**
>
> 1 C He's probably playing basketball right now.

Exam task

Students underline the key words in the sentences 1–7 first. As the students do this Exam task, remind them to underline the answers in the text and to write the question number next to it. Allow the students time to compare their answers in pairs first before checking the answers.

> **Answers**
>
> 1 C (He's probably playing basketball right now *but we don't know if he's winning*)
> 2 A (His collection includes shoes for playing tennis and basketball, and trainers for meeting his friends.)
> 3 B (Ben doesn't sell his shoes because he would like to be rich)
> 4 A (he gives a free pair to someone who hasn't got the money to buy them.)
> 5 B (It all started two years ago)
> 6 B (<u>Unlike</u> Ben, they have to play sports like basketball without shoes)
> 7 C (If you'd like more information about Ben ... visit the *SavesByB* website)

Writing

Part 9

1 Point out that Writing Part 9 is the last question on the Reading and Writing Paper. Here the students have to write a short email, note or message. Students have to answer three questions or content points and write 25–35 words.

> **Answers**
>
> 1 An email to Alice.   2 three: What are you wearing? What are you doing? Who are you with?   3 25–35 words

2 Remind the students of the criteria. Encourage the students to justify their choice of best answer and also why the other two answers are not good.

> **Answers**
>
> 2 is the best answer because it answers the three questions and it is between 25 and 35 words.

3 Before students read the teacher's comments, encourage them to think of what a teacher might write for each one.

> **Answers**
> a 3   b 1   c 2

Exam task

Read the Exam tip as a class. Ask the students to answer the three questions in Exercise 1 about this Exam task. (1 an email to Dan   2 three questions: What do you usually wear for school? What are your favourite kinds of clothes? What are you wearing now?   3 25–35 words)

> **Model answer**
>
> Hi Dan,
> We can wear what we like for school. My favourite clothes are jeans and T-shirts. Now, I'm wearing shorts because it's hot.
> See you soon,
> Michele

4 Before collecting in the students' writing, make sure they check their work by answering these questions.

Speaking

Part 2

1 Brainstorm what the students remember about Speaking Part 2 from Unit 3.

> **Suggested answer**
>
> Student A has got some information about a new sports shop and Student B has some question words. B has to ask some questions about the sports shop and A has to answer them.

2 Remind the students that they should write complete correct questions. Don't check the students' questions for now; they will listen and check in Exercise 4. Do the first one together as a class.

> **Suggested answers**
>
> 1 Where is the fashion show?   2 How can I get there?
> 3 When is the fashion show?   4 What can I see there?
> 5 How much is it?   6 How can I get some more information?

3 ⬤ 15 Encourage the students to justify their answers and then read the Exam tip as a class.

> **Answers**
>
> 1 No she doesn't. She just says the words on the question card.
> 2 Yes, he does. He answers in full sentences using the words on his information card.

> **Recording script**
>
> | | |
> |---|---|
> | Marina: | Date fashion show? |
> | Jon: | It's on Saturday 1st May. |
> | Marina: | Where fashion show? |
> | Jon: | It's at the Truman Centre. |
> | Marina: | What see? |
> | Jon: | You can see clothes made by young people. |
> | Marina: | Cost? |
> | Jon: | It's £2.50 for under 16s. |
> | Marina: | How get there? |
> | Jon: | You can take the bus or train. |
> | Marina: | More information? |
> | Jon: | You can call or text 6611. |

4 ⬤ 16 Ask the students why Kandela's questions are better than Marina's questions in Exercise 3.

> **Recording script**
>
> | | |
> |---|---|
> | Kandela: | (3) When is the fashion show? |
> | Jon: | It's on Saturday 1st May. |
> | Kandela: | (1) Where is the fashion show? |
> | Jon: | It's at the Truman Centre. |
> | Kandela: | (4) What can I see there? |
> | Jon: | You can see clothes made by young people. |
> | Kandela: | (5) How much is it? |
> | Jon: | It's £2.50 for under 16s. |
> | Kandela: | (2) How can I get there? |
> | Jon: | You can take the bus or train. |
> | Kandela: | (6) How can I get more information? |
> | Jon: | You can call or text 6611. |

Exam task

Students work in pairs. Read the full exam instructions for the sports shop. Give them three to four minutes to carry out the task.

Student A, here is some information about a new sports shop. Student B, you don't know anything about the new sports shop, so ask Student A some questions about it. Use these words to help you.

Pete's Sports Shop
55 Park Road
Tel: 658 224

We sell balls, rackets, clothes and more!
Monday – Saturday 9.30 a.m. – 5.00 p.m.

New Sports Shop

♦ name / shop ?

♦ open ?

♦ where ?

♦ what / buy ?

♦ more information ?

Then read them the exam instructions for the magazine:

Student B, here is some information about a new magazine. Student A, you don't know anything about the magazine so ask B some questions about it. Now A, ask B your questions and B, you answer them.

Teen Sports
A new magazine for teenagers

Only £1.75

Articles about sportspeople, new sports and more

On sale every Friday

www.TeenSports.com

Teen Sports

♦ for young people ?

♦ what / read about ?

♦ price ?

♦ when / buy ?

♦ more information ?

> **Suggested answer**
>
> What's the name of the new sports shop? / What's the sports shop called?
> It's (called) Pete's Sports Shop.
> When does it open? / When is it open?
> It's open Monday – Saturday 9.30 a.m. – 5 p.m.
> Where is it?
> It's at 55 Park Road.
> What can I buy there?
> You can buy balls, rackets, clothes and more.
> How can I get more information?
> The phone number is 658224
>
> Is the magazine for young people?
> Yes, it is. It's for teenagers.
> What can I read about?
> You can read articles about sportspeople, new sports and more.
> How much is it?
> It's only £1.75.
> When can I buy it?
> You can buy it every Friday.
> How can I get more information?
> You can visit www.TeenSports.com

5 Great places to visit

Unit objectives

KEY FOR SCHOOLS TOPICS	places & buildings, shopping
GRAMMAR	past simple positive, negative and questions, *ago*, time expressions *in / at / on*
VOCABULARY	places & building, days, months and dates
READING	Part 2: Trying all three answers in each space
WRITING	Part 9: Starting and finishing well
LISTENING	Part 5: Completing the information with a day or a date
SPEAKING	Part 1: Answering questions about the past, saying when with *in, at, on* + time expression

Places & buildings

Grammar & vocabulary

Vocabulary – Places

1 Have a brief class discussion on the places in their town using these questions: *Have you got these places in your town? What places do tourists usually visit? Where do you usually go with your friends / family?* Go over the words in the box. Check students' pronunciation. Ask them to tell you if these places are in their town.

Answers

2 museum   3 department store   4 theatre   5 police station
6 bookshop   7 university   8 newsagent

Grammar – Past simple positive

2 Encourage the students to look for clues, e.g. a capital city in Europe, he went to the Museum of Scotland.

Answers

He's in Edinburgh, Scotland. (I'm in a <u>capital city</u> in Europe, we went to the National Museum of <u>Scotland</u>)

3 If necessary, explain that we form regular verbs in the past by adding *–ed* to the verb. Other verbs are irregular and students need to learn these. (There is a list of irregular verbs at the back of their book). Remind students that the past simple form of *be* is *was* or *were*.

Answers

Underline: explored, stopped, didn't want, enjoyed, studied
Circle: got, had, was, went

4 Encourage the students to use the list of irregular verbs at the back of the book and the spelling rules of regular verbs in the Grammar reference on page 82 to help them do this exercise. Point out that the most common mistake is the past form of *cost*.

Answers

2 ~~enjoied~~ = enjoyed   3 ~~singed~~ = sang   4 ~~visitted~~ = visited
5 ~~stoped~~ = stopped   6 ~~costed~~ = cost

5 Students read the complete text before writing. Refer them to the list of irregular verbs and the Grammar reference on page 82 to check the past simple forms. Check spelling.

Answers

1 was   2 died   3 moved   4 found   5 was   6 decided
7 began   8 wrote   9 needed   10 tried   11 were   12 opened

> See the Workbook and CD ROM for further practice on Grammar & Vocabulary.

Reading

Part 2

Grammar – Past simple negative

1 Use the sentences in the exercise or alternatively, with books closed, write some false sentences on the board, e.g. *Levi Strauss was born in the USA* and ask the students to correct the sentences using the past simple negative.

Answers

1 wasn't, weren't   2 didn't + infinitive

2 Look at the notice for the school trip together as a class and ask the class some general comprehension questions, e.g. *Where are they going? When are they going? What do the students have to bring? How are they going? What time does the bus leave?* Then, ask the students to read Callum's email without writing and to find the differences between the information on the notice and the actual trip. Point out that the students need to complete the email using the past simple <u>negative</u>. Refer students to the Grammar reference on page 82.

Answers

1 wasn't   2 wasn't   3 didn't go   4 didn't have   5 didn't travel / didn't go   6 didn't make   7 didn't get

3 Remind the students that the instructions will tell them what the sentences are about.

Answers

1 five   2 a school trip   3 choose the best answer

4 Read the Exam tip as a class. Remind the students to look for verb + noun combinations in this part. Encourage the students to keep a list of these in their notebooks.

Answers

1 have   2 go   3 spent   4 take   5 had   6 took

Exam task

Encourage the students to read the five sentences first without writing. As they read they should try to think of a possible answer without looking at the three options. Finally, if they are still not sure, they should try all three answers in the space to see which sounds the best.

Answers

1 A 2 A 3 C 4 B 5 B

Further practice

Students write five sentences in the past simple about a school trip using the sentences in the Exam task as a model. In pairs, the students take turns to read out their sentences but leave a space in each one. Their partner has to guess the missing word, e.g. A: *Last week we went .... a school trip.* B: *Is it 'on'?*

Grammar & vocabulary

Vocabulary – Days & dates

1 & 2 Encourage students to make a guess at the answers using *I think it's ... because ...* . Ask the pair(s) of students with the most correct answers where they'd like to go for their prize – remind them it has to be a capital city.

Answers

1 A 2 B 3 A 4 A 5 C

3 If necessary, revise the spelling and pronunciation of days, months and dates in English. Remind students that although we say 'Wednesday the fifth of March', we usually write Wednesday 5th March without *the* or *of*.

Answers

March the thirty-first   Wednesday the fifth   the twentieth of August two thousand and seven   July nineteen ninety-eight Tuesday the third of February, twenty thirteen

Grammar – Past simple questions

4 Refer students to the Grammar reference on page 82.

Answers

1 (Question word) + *was/were* + *I, you, he*, etc.
2 (Question word) + *did* + *I, you, he*, etc. + infinitive

5 Explain these sentences should be questions in the past simple. Students ask and answer in pairs.

Answers

2 ~~Who you bought~~ your clothes with? = Who did you buy your clothes with?
3 I like your watch. How much ~~it cost~~? = How much did it cost?
4 ~~Have you take~~ photos last weekend? = Did you take photos last weekend?
5 What presents ~~do you get~~ on your last birthday? = What presents did you get on your last birthday?
6 Where ~~you stay~~ last holiday? = Where did you stay last holiday?

Grammar – *ago*

6 Write two or three true sentences about yourself on the board, e.g. *I started working in this school a / one year ago.; I went to New York six months ago.; I saw a good film at the cinema three days ago.* Then ask the students questions to check they understand the meaning of ago, e.g. *When did I start working here? (last year) When did I go to New York? (last September)*, etc. *What word do we use to tell us when something happened? (ago) Do we write it before or after the time? (after)* The students will need to look at their quiz answers in Exercise 2 again to do this exercise. Refer students to the Grammar reference on page 82.

Answers

1 1.5   2 20   3 50 (these answers are true for 2014)
We use *ago* e.g. 1½ centuries ago, 20 years ago, 50 months ago.

7 Point out that the students need to use the past simple + *ago* to say when they did it.

Suggested answers

I went shopping in a department store two weeks ago.
I played sport in a sports centre two days ago.
I saw a film in the cinema a week ago.
I bought something in an online shop a month ago.
I borrowed a book from the library three weeks ago.

Further practice

In pairs, students ask and answer questions about their sentences with follow-up questions, e.g. *When did you last go shopping in a department store? I went shopping in a department store two weeks ago. (Where? What did you buy?) When did you last play sport in a sports centre? I played sport in a sports centre two days ago. (What sport did you play? Did you win?)* etc.

> See the Workbook and CD ROM for further practice on Grammar & Vocabulary.

Listening

Part 5

1 Focus on the photo and ask the students to say where it was taken (Hollywood). Invite a brief discussion on what the students know about Hollywood, e.g. films are made there so many film stars live there, the Oscar ceremony is held there, etc.

Answers

1 Hollywood, California, USA.
2 The Dolby Theater is also a cinema; Lucky Devils is a restaurant; Hollywood Boulevard is a street; Staples Center is a sports stadium.

2 Ask students some questions about Listening Part 5, e.g. *How many people do they listen to in this part? (one) What do they need to complete? (some notes with information)*, etc. Then ask them to look at the Exam task and to tell you what this task is about (a tour for young people).

Answers

2 Address: 25, 709   3 Type of food: fast food, pizza   4 a sport: football, basketball   5 Price: $10, $20

3 🔲 **17** Read the Exam tip as a class. Point out that the students have to spell the days and months correctly. Encourage the students to predict possible answers before they listen. Point out that for each question they will hear two possible days, dates, numbers, etc., but only one is correct. With a stronger class, play the recording again and encourage the students to listen for the other word and to tell you what it refers to. (1 9th = Selena left for Los Angeles, 2 Monday = they left on Monday evening, 3 Friday = they did a Hollywood tour, 4 two = she started school two days ago).

Answers

1 5th   2 Tuesday   3 Saturday   4 four

Recording script

(1) My birthday was on 5th April but we didn't leave for Los Angeles until 9th April. I remember the day well. We left on Monday evening and (2) we got there on Tuesday morning. The flight took about 11 hours.

We were tired on the first day so we didn't do very much. We went on a Hollywood Tour on Friday but (3) the best day was Saturday because we saw the LA Lakers play a basketball match at Staples Center. (4) We got back four days ago and I started school again two days ago.

Exam task

🔲 **18** If appropriate, point out that the cost for this listening is in dollars ($). However, in the real exam, the price is always in pounds (£). Play the recording at least twice. Encourage the students to compare their answers in pairs before you tell them the correct answers.

Answers

1 23rd July / July 23rd (at 10 a.m.)   2 6000   3 burgers
4 basketball   5 27

Recording script

You will hear some information about a tour for young people.

Listen and complete each question.

Woman: Our Hollywood tour for young people is called *I love Hollywood*. Join us for an exciting day (1) on July 23rd at 10 a.m. We also have an adult tour on July 25th at 11 a.m.

(2) Meet at our office at 6000 Hollywood Boulevard. Hollywood Boulevard is home to famous Hollywood cinemas. But of course in America we don't say cinema, we say theater. We will visit the Dolby Theater at 6801 Hollywood Boulevard and the Chinese Theater which is next to it.

Next (3) we'll have burgers at Lucky Devils Restaurant. Maybe we'll see somebody famous there, but a lot of the stars prefer to eat salad and healthy food in Beverly Hills.

In the afternoon, (4) we'll take a short bus trip to the stadium where California's best basketball team plays. As part of the tour of their stadium, you will watch one of their matches. Sorry, we don't have tickets for baseball or American football matches.

The price for this very special tour is $37 for adults and (5) $27 for under 16s. We suggest you book your place soon as this tour is very popular.

---

4 & 5 Ask the students to read the competition questions again and tell them that they should model their own questions on these. If necessary, write two or three questions together as a class. If appropriate, set up Exercise 5 as a class competition or a quiz show. Divide the class into teams; the teams take turns to ask their questions and answer the other teams' questions. Award 1 point for a correct question and 1 point for a correct answer.

Suggested answers

1 When did the department store first open?
   A 1995   B 1998   C 2000
2 What did Messi buy when he visited the store?
   A a football   B some shoes   C a shirt
3 When did the pizza restaurant open?
   A April 2012   B May 2012   C June 2012

🌑 **CLIL** Geography: In small groups, students plan a tour of their own town for tourists. Each group should think of a date for the tour, a place to meet, somewhere to have lunch, a place to go in the afternoon and the price. Then they should prepare a short description of their tour with a map. Each group takes turns to read their tour description. The others listen and write down the key information, i.e. the date, meeting place, lunch, afternoon visit and price.

Shopping

Writing

Part 9

1 Have a brief classroom discussion on shopping using these questions: *1 Do you like shopping? Why (not)? 2 What kinds of things do you enjoy buying? 3 Did you buy anything last weekend? What did you buy?* Then brainstorm a list of different kinds of shops. Encourage the students to justify their answers, e.g. *I think they went to a clothes shop because I can see some new clothes.*

Suggested answers

They went to a clothes shop (clothes), a bookshop (books), a chemist (toothbrush, toothpaste & shampoo), a supermarket (food), a sports shop (tennis racket and balls), a DVD shop (DVDs), a newsagent (a newspaper), the post office (a parcel).

2 Encourage the students to justify their answer.

Suggested answers

I think she's feeling a little angry because she waited for her friend but she didn't come.

3 Ask the students to think of a suitable reply to Petra's email before they read the answers.

Answers

2 This is better because it starts and finishes well.

4 Read the Exam tip as a class. Ask the students to cover the exercise and then think of ways they can start and finish a note, email or postcard. Students open their books and check their ideas.

Answers

Starting: Hello; Dear John
Finishing: See you soon; Bye for now

Exam task

Ask the class to read the Exam task. Encourage the students to say what the difference is between this Writing Part 9 task and the Unit 4 Writing task. (Here the students are told what to write in bullet points whereas in Unit 4 they have to answer an email or message. In both tasks however, they need to answer three questions or content points and write 25–35 words). The students then answer these questions: *How can you start and finish this email? (Hi Zoe, Best wishes) What three pieces of information do you need to include? (Who you went shopping with, what you bought and what you did afterwards.) What words or expressions from this unit can you use? (go shopping, have a good time, take the lift, supermarket, chemist, etc.).*

Model answer

Hi Zoe,
I went shopping with my cousin yesterday. We had a great time in the department store. I bought some new jeans. Afterwards, we took the lift to the sixth floor and we had a drink in the café.
Bye for now,
Kath

5 Remind the students that they should always check their work carefully before they finish.

Speaking

Part 1

Grammar – Time expressions: *in / at / on*

1 With books closed, begin this section by writing the two questions on the board: *Where did you go last weekend? What did you do?* In pairs, students take turns to ask and answer the questions. They then work in the same pairs to answer the questions in the exercise.

Answers

1 She went to Singapore.
2 She visited the Science museum, she went shopping and they explored the Bird Park.

2 Ask the students to underline the examples of *in*, *at* or *on* with a time expression in the blog.

Answers

1 on 2 in 3 at

Further practice

Read out these time expressions and ask the students for the correct preposition: *7 March, the weekend, 2011, 26 May 1999, the evening, October, 10.45.*

3 Elicit some questions as a class. Do not answer the questions now; the students will do this in the Exam task.

Suggested answers

1 Where did you eat on Tuesday?
2 Where did you go in the evening?
3 What did you do at 6.30 p.m. yesterday?
4 When did you eat on Tuesday?

4 ⊙ 19 Point out that the examiner may ask questions about the past in Part 1. (In Part 2, the candidates usually ask and answer questions in the present). Play the recording and remind the students they will have to justify their answers, e.g. *I think the girl/boy (doesn't) answer(s) the question well because …*

Answers

The girl answers the questions well because she uses complete sentences in the past simple.
The boy doesn't answer well. He answers with words and not complete sentences.

Recording script

1

Examiner:	What did you do yesterday after school?
Girl:	I went to the sports centre.
Examiner:	What did you have for dinner?
Girl:	We had soup and bread.
Examiner:	What time did you go to bed?
Girl:	I went to bed at ten o'clock.
Examiner:	Thank you.

2

Examiner:	What did you do yesterday after school?
Boy:	Go library, do homework.
Examiner:	What did you have for dinner?
Boy:	Pasta.
Examiner:	What time did you go to bed?
Boy:	In ten o'clock.
Examiner:	Thank you.

---

5 Read the Exam tip as a class. Remind the students that the examiner is asking questions about yesterday so the boy's answers need to be in the past.

Answers

2 I had pasta for dinner.
3 I went to bed at 10 o'clock.

Exam task

Encourage the pairs to take turns to be Student A and Student B. Remind Student A to ask questions about the past and Student B to answer using the past and *in*, *at* and *or*.

Suggested answer

A: Where did you eat on Tuesday?
B: I ate at home with my family on Tuesday.
A: Where did you go in the evening?
B: I went home and I did my homework in the evening.
A: What did you do at 6.30 p.m. yesterday?
B: I finished my homework and then we had dinner at 8 o'clock.

Getting there

Unit objectives

KEY FOR SCHOOLS TOPICS	transport, travel
GRAMMAR	comparative & superlative adjectives
VOCABULARY	transport, places, giving directions
READING	Part 3b: Reading what the person says before and after the space
WRITING	Part 7: Looking for words that go together
LISTENING	Part 2: Choosing the correct answer
SPEAKING	Part 2: Asking your partner to repeat a question, saying a question in a different way

Transport

Grammar & vocabulary

Vocabulary – Transport

1 The words in the suggested answers below are the transport words on the Key for Schools Vocabulary list. (This list is published by Cambridge English as a guide to the vocabulary needed to prepare students for the exam. It can be downloaded for free from the Cambridge English website – www.cambridgeenglish.org). (There is also a skateboard and a balloon in the picture.)

> **Suggested answers**
>
> Sea: boat
> Land: lorry, tram, train, motorbike, bike, bus, car, coach, taxi
> Air: plane, helicopter

2 Ask the students to think about the types of transport we use with these verbs first, e.g. *drive + car*, *lorry* and *bus*; *sail + boat*, *ship*, etc.

> **Answers**
>
> 2 fly   3 walk   4 ride   5 sail

Grammar – Comparative adjectives

3 Encourage students to make a guess and then to check their answers. Then ask them to underline the examples of comparative adjectives in the exercise and answer these questions: *Do we use comparative adjectives to compare two or three things?* (*two things*) *What do we add to short adjectives?* (*-er*) *What word do we add to longer adjectives?* (*more*) *What other word do we use with comparative adjectives?* (*than*) *Does it go before or after the adjective?* (*after*).

> **Answers**
>
> 1 busier   2 bigger   3 nearer to   4 more expensive
> 5 quieter   6 faster

4 Ask the students to look at the spelling rules for comparative adjectives in the Grammar reference on page 83 before they do this exercise.

> **Answers**
>
> 2 ~~beautifuller~~ than = more beautiful than   3 ~~beeter~~ = better
> 4 ~~more far~~ = farther / further   5 ~~more easy~~ = easier
> 6 ~~biger~~ = bigger

5 Encourage the students to read the complete text before they start writing. Check that the students spell the comparative adjectives correctly.

> **Answers**
>
> 2 faster   3 more expensive   4 bigger   5 more modern
> 6 cheaper   7 healthier (or *more healthy*)   8 quicker   9 drier

Further practice

In pairs, students write about transport in their town.

> See the Workbook and CD ROM for further practice on Grammar & Vocabulary.

Listening

Part 2

1 Refer students to the Exam task. This is the first time they have seen this type of task in this book so make sure they understand what they have to do. Then ask students to look at the picture. Point out that we say *go by train, bus, car*, etc. but *go on foot*.

> **Answers**
>
> How did B get to the cinema? She went by bus, she didn't go by bike.
> How did C get to the cinema? She went on foot, she didn't go by bike.

2 🔊 20 Read the Exam tip as a class. Point out that the students will hear both answers, A & B, in this exercise but only one of them is correct. If necessary, play the recording twice. With a stronger class, ask the students to say if the correct answer is the first or second expression they hear.

> **Answers**
>
> 1 B   2 B   3 A

> **Recording script**
>
> | Mum: | Did you have a good time at the cinema? |
> | Natalie: | Yeah but my friends were late. Sandra missed the bus so (1) <u>she went on foot</u>. |
> | Mum: | Really? What about Dina? Did she walk too? |
> | Natalie: | No, she had lunch late so (2) <u>she borrowed her brother's bike</u>. |
> | Mum: | And Maria? She's always early. |
> | Natalie: | Not this time. (3) <u>She took the bus</u>. I told her it was quicker to cycle but she didn't listen. |

3 Point out that the students need to write the answers on the pictures in Exercise 2. Play the recording again if necessary.

Answers

A Dina   B Maria   C Sandra

Exam task

🔴 21 Ask the students to read through the lists of people (1–5) and transport (A–H) first. Encourage the students to think about what verbs they are likely to hear with each transport word, e.g. *go by train* or *bus*, *ride a bike*, etc. After completing the task, hand out photocopies of the recording script on page 95. Students underline the correct answers.

Answers

1 F   2 H   3 E   4 C   5 D

Recording script

Listen to Ethan talking to his mum about his family.

How are Ethan's family getting to his birthday party?

For questions 1–5 write a letter A–H next to each person.

Ethan:	I'm home! Where are you?
Mum:	Hi, Ethan! I'm in the kitchen. Happy Birthday!
Ethan:	Thanks mum! But where is everyone else? Why are they so late for my party?
Mum:	Well, your sister has football practice until 6.00 p.m. (0) Then she's coming home by bus.
Ethan:	Why doesn't she take the tram? It's much faster. And where's Dad?
Mum:	He phoned fifteen minutes ago. Your grandma missed the half past five bus so (1) your dad is going to drive her.
Ethan:	Is Granddad coming in Dad's car, too?
Mum:	He had to work this afternoon (2) so he's going to take the underground. It's probably quicker than the car, anyway.
Ethan:	I can hear a motorbike. Is that Uncle Tom?
Mum:	I spoke to him this morning. (3) He's going to take a taxi after his meeting.
Ethan:	Is Ursula coming with him? Or is she taking the underground?
Mum:	(4) Your cousin Ursula's cycling here right now. She'll be here in ten minutes. Don't worry!
Ethan:	Great! Who else is coming?
Mum:	My sister!
Ethan:	Aunt May?
Mum:	Yes, (5) she's getting the tram from her house to the train station at the end of our road.
Ethan:	Mum! What's that noise in the living room?
Voices:	Surprise! Happy Birthday ...

---

4 Encourage the students to answer with complete sentences and to say why.

Suggested answers

How do you go to sports practice? My friend's dad sometimes drives us because it's faster than going by bus. When the weather's good, we go by bike because it's healthier.
How do you go to your friend's house? I usually walk because he lives very near and so it's quicker than going by car.
How do you go to the town centre? I usually go by bus. Sometimes my mother drives me.

Reading

Part 3b

Vocabulary – Directions

1 Have a brief class discussion on whether the students enjoy playing video games and which games they would recommend. Tell the students that they are going to read a review of a new video game

Suggested answers

I'd like to play it because I like playing video games.

2 Encourage the students to try to complete the exercise first before you help them with the meaning of the words. Check that the students pronounce the words correctly.

Answers

2 crossing   3 roundabout   4 car park   5 square   6 bridge

3 Encourage students to read the conversations quickly to get a general idea and to match them with the pictures without completing them. (They'll do this in Exercise 4).

Answers

1 B   2 C   3 A

4 Point out that, apart from question 1 (supermarket) and 5 (park), the students need to use the words in Exercise 2. Then students underline the useful expressions to give directions, e.g. *behind, near, over the bridge, opposite, go over, turn right at, cross the road at, it's on your left.*

Answers

2 town square   3 bridge   4 sports centre   5 park   6 roundabout
7 traffic lights   8 crossing

5 Encourage the students to use some of the expressions in Exercise 3 in their conversations.

Suggested answers

Where's the town square? It's opposite the supermarket.
Where's the library? Go over the roundabout. Turn right at the traffic lights and it's at the crossing opposite the train station.
Where's the park? Go over the bridge. It's opposite the sports centre, next to the school.
Where's the sports centre? Go over the bridge. It's opposite the school and the park.
Where's the supermarket? It's in front of the car park and the town square.

6 Ask the students to read the Exam task and to say what they have to do in this part. Explain this is the second part of the Reading Part 3 task. (Reading Part 3a was in units 2 & 5).

Encourage a brief class discussion on what they can see in the photo (two children talking together). Ask the students to read the children's conversation (without writing) and to tell you what they are talking about (they're making plans).

Suggested answer

It's over the bridge and opposite the park.

7 Students read the choices and choose the answer closest to their suggestions in Exercise 6. Elicit what questions could come before A (*What time shall we meet?*) and C (*What's the shop like?*).

Answer

B

8 Encourage the students to think of their own answer before they read the three possible answers (A–C).

Answer

Yes, all three answers are possible.

Elicit which word in Nick's answers helps them to find the answer (4.00 p.m.). Read the Exam tip as a class.

Answer

B

See the Workbook and CD ROM for further practice.

Exam task

Students read the complete conversation first to get a general idea. Then, they should read it again and think of their own possible answers. Finally, they should look for the correct possible answer making sure they read what the person says before and after the space. Remind students to cross out the answers as they use them.

Answers

1 B 2 F 3 A 4 H 5 E

Further practice

In pairs, students use Jack and Amy's conversation as a model for a conversation making plans, using the same questions.

Travel

Writing

Part 7

Grammar – Superlative adjectives

1 Revise the vocabulary from the previous page (*traffic lights, roundabout, bridge, crossing*, etc.) and encourage the students to talk about what they can see in the photo.

Suggested answer

It's a busy crossing in Asia (because of the writing).

2 Encourage the students to say what other information they find out about the Shibuya crossing, e.g. *hundreds of people*

cross the road every time the lights change, there's a statue of a dog, many young people meet there. Have a brief class discussion on famous landmarks in their town, e.g. a town square, a shopping centre, a large roundabout, etc.

Answers

It's Shibuya crossing in Japan.

3 Students underline the examples of the superlative adjectives in Exercise 2 and say what the difference is between comparative and superlative adjectives, e.g. we use superlative adjectives to compare one thing with many things (comparative adjectives compare two things), we add *the ... -est* to short adjectives (with comparatives, we add *-er* and *than*) and we usually add *the most* to longer adjectives (*more* to comparative adjectives). Refer students to the spelling rules for superlative adjectives in the Grammar reference on page 83 before they do this. Check the students' spelling. Then put students into teams and give them a few minutes to memorise the information. With books closed, ask each team a question, e.g. *What is the longest bridge in the world? Where is it? How long is it?* etc.

Answers

2 The longest 3 The biggest 4 the oldest 5 the worst

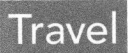 **CLIL** Geography (Web page): In small groups, the students look for information about superlative places, buildings, transport, etc. in the world, e.g. the widest bridge, the biggest park, etc. The students then write a web page for the other groups. When the groups have found the answers, they make a poster to illustrate some of the superlative things they have found.

4 Remind the students that in this part, they have to complete each gap in a text with one word. Read the Exam tip as a class. Remind the students to read the complete sentence before they start writing.

Answers

1 most 2 than 3 are 4 not 5 to 6 were

Exam task

Students read the complete email first. Ask some general questions, e.g. *Where is Yasmin? How did she get there? What's the place like?* etc., before they start writing.

Answers

1 are 2 by 3 to 4 the 5 most 6 ago 7 lot 8 than
9 There 10 did (*accept* could)

See the Workbook and CD ROM for further practice.

Speaking

Part 2

1 Ask students to tell you what they remember about Speaking Part 2 first. Then in pairs, students discuss the questions. Encourage them to justify their answers.

Suggested answer

I would like to go on the tour because it looks exciting and interesting but I think I'll be a little frightened, too.

2 Remind the students that in Speaking Part 2, they will be given questions prompts like these but they will need to produce complete questions to do well in this part.

Answers

2 How much is it? / How much does it cost? / What's the price?   3 Is it open every day? / Can I do it every day?
4 What can I see?   5 How can I get more information? What's the telephone number?

3 🔘 22 If necessary, play the recording twice. Encourage the students to tell you if Marco and Lucia do the task well (Yes, they do. Lucia doesn't always understand Marco's questions but this doesn't matter because she asks him to repeat the question).

Answers

1 Where is the helicopter tour?
2 a How much does the tour cost? b Is it expensive?
3 a Is there a tour every day? b Can I go on the tour on Fridays?
4 What can I see on the tour?
5 a How can I get more information? b Is there a telephone number?

Recording script

Examiner:	Lucia, here is some information about a helicopter tour. Marco, you don't know anything about the helicopter tour, so ask Lucia some questions about it. Use these words to help you. Do you understand?
Marco:	Yes, of course.
Examiner:	Now, Marco, ask Lucia your questions about the helicopter tour and Lucia, you answer them.
Marco:	(1) Where is the helicopter tour?
Lucia:	It's in Sydney, Australia.
Marco:	(2a) How much does the tour cost?
Lucia:	Can you repeat that, please?
Marco:	(2b) Is it expensive?
Lucia:	No, it's only $99 per person.
Marco:	(3a) Is there a tour every day?
Lucia:	Sorry, I don't understand.
Marco:	(3b) Can I go on the tour on Fridays?
Lucia:	No. It's on Saturdays and Sundays.
Marco:	(4) What can I see on the tour?
Lucia:	You can see Sydney Harbour Bridge, the Opera House and more from the air.
Marco:	(5a) How can I get more information?
Lucia:	Sorry?
Marco:	(5b) Is there a telephone number?
Lucia:	Yes, you can call or text 456772.
Marco:	Thank you.

---

4 Read the Exam tip as a class. Remind the students that they can ask their partner to repeat a question as Lucia does.

Answers

3 Can I go on the tour on Fridays?
5 Is there a telephone number?

Exam task

Read the full instructions to the class. Remind the students to ask their partners to repeat a question if they don't understand. Make sure students have their books open at the correct pages.

Student A, here is some information about a boat tour. Student B, you don't know anything about the boat tour so ask A some questions about it. Now B, ask your questions about the boat tour and A, you answer them.

Boat Tours
Bangkok, Thailand

Tuesday – Sunday
Only $40 per person (Tickets on sale opposite market)
Bring hat and comfortable shoes
Visit www.boattours.com for more information

Boat Tours

♦ cost ? $?

♦ every day ?

♦ where / buy tickets ?

♦ website ?

♦ what / wear ?

Student B, here is some information about a transport museum. Student A, you don't know anything about the transport museum so ask B some questions about it. Now A, ask B your questions and B, you answer them.

James Hall Transport Museum
Johannesburg, South Africa

The largest transport museum in Africa!
Motorbikes, trams, fire engines and more!
Tuesday – Friday 9.00 a.m. – 5.00 p.m.
Entrance is free!
Call 456822

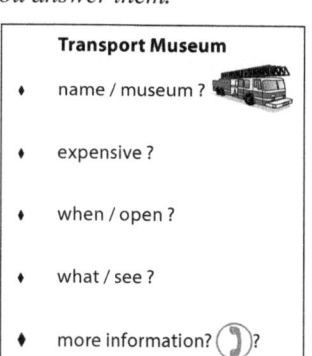

Transport Museum

♦ name / museum ?

♦ expensive ?

♦ when / open ?

♦ what / see ?

♦ more information? 📞 ?

Suggested answers

B: How much does the boat tour cost?
A: It's only $40 per person.
B: Can I do the boat tour every day?
A: No, you can do it Tuesday to Sunday.
B: Where can I buy tickets?
A: The tickets are on sale opposite the market.
B: Is there a website?
A: Yes. It's w-w-w dot boattours dot com
B: What do I have to wear?
A: Bring a hat and comfortable shoes.
B: Thanks!

A: What's the name of the museum?
B: It's called the James Hall Transport Musuem.
A: Is it expensive?
B: It's free!
A: When does it open?
B: It opens at 9 am but only Tuesday to Friday.
A: What can I see there?
B: You can see motorbikes, trams, fire engines and more.
A: What's the phone number?
B: It's 456822.
A: Thank you!

7 School rules!

Unit objectives

KEY FOR SCHOOLS TOPICS	school & study, entertainment
GRAMMAR	*must / mustn't, should / shouldn't, can / could*, adverbs of manner
VOCABULARY	school subjects, musical instruments
READING	Part 1: Looking for words with a similar meaning
WRITING	Part 9: Checking spelling before finishing
LISTENING	Part 5: Choosing the correct answer
SPEAKING	Part 1: Answering questions about school and study

School & study

Grammar & vocabulary

Vocabulary – Education

1 Focus students' attention on the picture and encourage them to say what this unit is about, i.e. schools, classrooms, rules, school subjects, etc. With a stronger class, encourage the students to read the sentences and write the school subject without looking at the words given. If you wish, brainstorm more school subjects, e.g. P.E. / sport, French, Spanish, religion, biology, etc. Students will talk about the subjects they study at school in the Speaking section of this unit.

Answers

2 art   3 music   4 history   5 English   6 science   7 geography

2 After checking answers as a class, students work in pairs taking turns to ask and answer the questions.

Answers

1 teach   2 miss   3 take   4 learn   5 spend

Grammar – *must / mustn't*

3 If necessary, pre-teach 'school rule' by giving some examples, e.g. *Do you have to wear a school uniform? Can you eat in class?* Students underline the words, then say what word we use to talk about rules and obligation (*must*). Focus on the form by asking questions, e.g. *What is the negative form of 'must'?* (*mustn't*) *Is 'must' followed by the –ing form or the infinitive?* (infinitive without *to*) *Do we use 'must' for all persons, I, you, he, etc?* (Yes)

Answers

1 No, she can't. (We <u>must wear jackets</u> and tights all year, even in the <u>summer</u>.)
2 No, they can't. (You <u>mustn't</u> walk or <u>sit on the grass in winter</u>)

4 Encourage the students to read the complete sentences first before they start writing. Refer students to the Grammar reference on page 84.

Answers

2 mustn't use   3 mustn't take   4 must wear
5 must walk   6 mustn't listen

Further practice

With students at the same school, students write some school rules for a perfect school. If they go to different schools, they write their real school rules and then find out who goes to the strictest school.

Grammar – *should / shouldn't*

5 Ask the students to underline the words in the conversation which say it's a good idea (*should*) and it isn't a good idea (*shouldn't*) to do something. Highlight the form of *should* either by referring the students to the Grammar reference on page 84 or by asking questions, e.g. *What's the negative form of should?* (shouldn't) *What form of the verb follows 'should'?* (the infinitive without *to*) *Do we use the same form of 'should' for all persons?* (Yes). After checking the answers, invite a brief classroom discussion on whether the students agree with the boy.

Answers

1 Yes   2 No

6 This exam advice has been taken from the Examiner's Report for the *Key for Schools* exams (see www.cambridgeenglish.org).

Answers

2 shouldn't do; should take   3 should read; should look
4 should answer; shouldn't leave   5 should check   6 shouldn't write; should use

See the Workbook and CD ROM for further practice on Grammar & Vocabulary.

Reading

Part 1

1 Encourage the students to look at the Exam task and to say what they have to do. Ask where in a school they would find these notices (A library B school snack shop C sports hall D reception E outside classroom F corridor G playground H school entrance). Read through the Exam tip as a class. Point out that the students need to look for words which have a similar meaning in the notices, rather than the same words. Make sure they underline the important words only and not every word.

Answers

2 You should <u>bring</u> your <u>teacher</u> a <u>note</u> if you <u>miss a class</u>. b (should write to the school)
3 <u>No ball</u> games. a (shouldn't play football)
4 <u>No running inside</u> the building. a (must walk at all times in the school)

Exam task

Remind the students to look for words which have a similar meaning and to cross out the answer when they find it.

Answers

1 E (shouldn't speak = be quiet)
2 B (Cans; cheaper = cold drinks half price)
3 C (If girls want to get dressed; need to go somewhere else = Boys' changing room)
4 G (mustn't play football = No ball games)
5 A (Put; back in right place = return all; correct shelf)

When you have checked the answers, ask students to work in small groups and write a list of similar notices in their school(s), e.g. *Boys' and Girls' Changing Rooms, No running, Turn off all mobile phones, Be quiet, English class, Speak English!* etc.

Entertainment

Grammar & vocabulary

Vocabulary – Musical instruments

1 Encourage the students to think of some more musical instruments.

Suggested answer

I can see a piano, a drum, a keyboard and what's this? I think it's a violin. (Other instruments include: guitar, clarinet, recorder, saxophone, xylophone.)

2 Ask the students to look at the picture first and to try to predict the answer before they read the text.

Answer

She teaches music in the town's music school.

Grammar – *can / could*

3 Point out that the students should underline the answers in the text. Encourage the students to say which word we use to talk about ability in the present (*can / can't* + infinitive) and which word we use to talk about ability in the past (*could / couldn't* + infinitive). If necessary, refer the students to the table in the Grammar reference on page 84.

Answers

1 Yes, when she was eleven. (When Camila was eleven, <u>she could play the violin well</u>)
2 Because they don't have enough money to buy them. (<u>Most of her students can't buy</u> their own instruments because <u>they don't have enough money</u>)

4 Encourage the students to read the complete email before they start writing.

Answers

2 can't sing   3 can learn   4 could sing   5 couldn't play
6 can write   7 can sing

5 Remind the students they need to use questions and answers with *can* and *could*. Brainstorm some questions and write them on the board first.

Suggested questions and answers

Can you play an instrument? Yes, I can. I can play the violin.
When did you start learning the violin? I could play it when I was 7.
Can anyone in your family play an instrument? Yes, my brother can play the piano and my mum can play the violin like me.

See the Workbook and CD ROM for further practice on Grammar & Vocabulary.

Listening

Part 5

Grammar – Adverbs of manner

1 Students can discuss who they think it is in pairs. Alternatively, with books closed, read the text sentence by sentence and students try to guess the famous person.

Answers

It's Leonardo da Vinci.

2 If necessary, point out that we use adverbs to describe how we do things (the verb). Ask students to say how we form adverbs in English (usually the adjective + *ly*) and point out that there are some irregular adverbs e.g. *good – well*.

Answers

1 badly   2 well   3 beautifully

3 Students look at the spelling rules for adverbs in the Grammar reference on page 84 before they do this exercise.

Answers

2 ~~wonderful~~ = wonderfully   3 ~~easly~~ = easily   4 ~~fastly~~ = fast
5 ~~bad~~ = badly   6 ~~good~~ = well

CLIL Art: In small groups, the students use the Internet to find some information about a famous artist. Then they prepare a short presentation for the class using PowerPoint. They should use *can / could* and adverbs in their presentation.

4 23 Ask the students to look at the Exam task and to say what they have to do in this part (complete some notes). Read the Exam tip together as a class, pointing out that although they may hear two possible answers, only one is correct. Play each recording twice. With a stronger class, encourage the students to say what the incorrect answer refers to (1a bring your instrument on Thursday; 2b I really enjoy history but ...; 3b a very important visitor is coming; 4a price in the bookshop; 5a we went there last year).

Answers

1 b   2 a   3 a   4 b   5 b

Recording script

Speaker one

So, bring your instruments on Thursday for the final practice before the school concert. Remember (1) <u>the concert is next Monday</u>.

Speaker two

I really enjoy my history class because the teacher is very good but (2) <u>I think I like geography best</u> because I like learning about different countries and people from those places.

Speaker three

Listen carefully please. (3) <u>Today your maths class will be one hour earlier at a quarter past eleven</u> because later at twelve fifteen, we've got a very important visitor from the music school.

Speaker four

You all need to buy this book for your English class. The price is £4.99 in the bookshop but we are selling it here (4) <u>in the school for the cheaper price of £3.50</u>.

Speaker five

This year (5) <u>we're going to the zoo with our science teacher</u>. I don't know why we can't go to the water park again. We had a great time there last year.

Exam task

🔘 **24** Ask the students to read the Exam task and say what the recording is about. (A teacher is giving a new class some information.) Encourage the students to say what type of information is missing in each space. (1 a time; 2 a phone number; 3 a school subject; 4 type of shoes; 5 price). Play the recording at least twice.

Answers

1 9.15   2 7885421   3 maths   4 trainers   5 £9.75

Further practice

Write on the board: *1 Is the Leonardo Da Vinci School of Art and Drama different to your school? How? 2 Would you like to study there? Why (not)? 3 What would you like to study there? 4 What would you not like to study?* In pairs, students take turns to ask and answer these questions.

Recording script

You will hear a teacher talking to her new class.

Listen and complete each question.

Hello and welcome to your first day at the Leonardo Da Vinci School of Art and Drama. (0) <u>My name's Amy Bird and I'm your teacher</u> for this year.

I'd like you to listen carefully to this important information. You must all be here in the classroom at nine o'clock every morning. I will check your names and (1) <u>the first class begins at a quarter past nine</u>.

If you can't come to school, your parents should write a note or they can call here (2) <u>on seven-double eight-five-four-two-one</u>. You must try to do all the work you miss. Ask a classmate for their phone number so you can call them.

In the mornings, you will all be together in this classroom for (3) <u>English, maths, and science</u>. In the afternoon, those of you on the Art programme will do art and music and those of you on the Drama programme will do dance and drama.

(4) <u>For your afternoon classes, you should wear trainers</u>. You can't dance, sing or act well if you're wearing uncomfortable boots, can you?

And finally, we have school sweaters which are for sale in reception. The normal price is twelve pounds fifty but (5) <u>they're only nine pounds seventy-five for those in their first year at the school</u>.

I think that's all for now. Any questions?

Speaking

Part 1

1 Invite a brief class discussion on whether any of the students have been to an International Summer School, perhaps to study English. Then ask them to work in pairs to think of questions they would ask in a similar situation.

Suggested answers

Where do you live?
What school do you go to?
What's your school like?
What subjects do you study?
Do you study English?

2 🔘 **25** Play the recording twice. The first time, the students put a tick next to the questions they hear from Exercise 1. On the second listening, stop the recording after each question so the students have time to write it down.

Answers

1 What's your name?   2 How do you spell it?   3 Where do you come from?   4 Do you study English at school?   5 What subjects do you study?   6 Which subjects do you like best?

Recording script

Wayne: Hi, I'm Wayne. (1) <u>What's your name?</u>

Flor: Hi, I'm Flor.

Wayne: That's an unusual name. (2) <u>How do you spell it?</u>

Flor: F-L-O-R. It's a Spanish name. I'm from Argentina. (3) <u>Where do you come from?</u>

Wayne: I'm from Capetown in South Africa. You can speak English really well. (4) <u>Do you study English at school?</u>

Flor: Yes, we have English on Tuesdays and Thursdays. We also do our history lessons in English. (5) <u>What subjects do you study?</u>

Wayne: Oh, the usual subjects like maths, English, science ... we also study French. (6) <u>Which subjects do you like best?</u>

Flor: I love art and music. That's why I'm here at this summer school. What about you?

Wayne: I love maths and computers so I'm going to do the computer course.

Flor: Really? I don't like computers very much and I'm terrible at maths.

3 Point out that in Speaking Part 1, the examiner will ask each candidate very similar questions to these.

Suggested answers

1 What's your name? I'm Maria.
2 How do you spell it? It's M-A-R-I-A.
3 Where do you come from? I come from Portugal.
4 Do you study English at school? Yes, I do.
5 What subjects do you study? I study maths, geography, history, science, etc.
6 Which subjects do you like best? I like geography best.

4 🔘 26 Point out that Carla and Jon are not asked exactly the same questions.

Answers

	Carla	Jon	Both
1			✓
2		✓	
3	✓		
4			✓

Recording script

Examiner: (1) Carla, do you study English at school?
Carla: Yes, I do. We have English on Mondays, Wednesdays and Fridays.
Examiner: (3) Which subjects do you like best?
Carla: I like art and music.
Examiner: Why?
Carla: Because I'm good at drawing. I like music because I can play the piano well.
Examiner: (4) What do you like about your school?
Carla: I've got a lot of friends there and the teachers are very friendly.
Examiner: Thank you. (1) Do you study English at school, Jon?
Jon: Yes, and I also go to a language school in the afternoon.
Examiner: (2) What other subjects do you study?
Jon: I study maths, art, music, history, science ...
Examiner: (4) What do you like about your school?
Jon: My friends.
Examiner: Why?
Jon: Because we have a lot of fun together.

---

5 Ask the students to say why Carla and Jon give good answers (because they answer in complete sentences and not just one or two words). Read the Exam tip together as a class. Point out that the missing words are all verbs.

Answers

Carla: 2 like   3 can play   4 've got
Jon: 5 study   6 have

Exam task

Remind the students to answer in full sentences and to take turns to be the examiner and the students.

Suggested answers

Examiner: Do you study English at school?
Student: Yes, I do. We have English four times a week.
Examiner: What other subjects do you study?
Student: I also study maths, geography, history, music, etc.
Examiner: What subjects do you like best?
Student: Sports.
Examiner: Why?
Student: Because I like playing football and basketball.
Examiner: What do you like about your school?
Student: I know all the other students there.

Writing

Part 9

1 Encourage the students to say what they can see in the picture first and what they think the boy is writing in his email.

Suggested answers

A little worried because he's performing the next day (I'm singing and dancing in our school show tomorrow and I'm a little worried.)

2 Ask the students to underline Sasha's three questions in his email first.

Suggested answers

Has your school got an end of year show? No, it hasn't.
Can you sing or dance well? I think I can sing quite well.
What other things do you do at the end of the year? We go on a school trip.

3 Read the Exam tip as a class first. Point out that these are some of the most common spelling mistakes that Key exam students make.

Answers

2 abaut = about   3 becouse = because   4 Tommorow = Tomorrow   5 o'clok = o'clock   6 beatiful = beautiful   7 withe = with   8 Bey = Bye

4 Also ask the students how many words they need to write in Writing Part 9 (25–35 words).

Answers

1 an email   2 What is your school like? What subjects do you like best? Who is your favourite teacher?

Exam task

Brainstorm some possible answers to the questions before the students start writing.

Model answer

Hi Jo
We have to study a lot at my school because we do a lot of exams. My favourite subjects are maths and science. I think my maths teacher is amazing.
Bye for now,

5 Remind the students that they should always leave time to check their work before they finish.

8 We had a great time!

Unit objectives

KEY FOR SCHOOLS TOPICS	holidays, personal experiences
GRAMMAR	past continuous, past simple & past continuous
VOCABULARY	holiday activities, adjectives of opinion
READING	Part 4: Choosing A, B or C correctly
WRITING	Part 8: Choosing the correct word, thinking about why the other word is wrong
LISTENING	Part 2: Listening for similar words
SPEAKING	Part 2: Answering in full sentences

Holidays

Grammar & vocabulary

Vocabulary – Holiday activities

1 Students take turns to ask and answer the questions in the quiz. Demonstrate this with a strong student, e.g.

Teacher: *When you're on holiday, do you prefer to A visit new countries? B visit your own country? or C stay at home?*

Student: *I prefer to visit new countries.*

2 Students can find the quiz results at the back of the Student's Book on page 127. Ask the students if they agree with the results.

3 Encourage the students to read the complete sentences first before they start writing.

> **Answers**
>
> 2 speak   3 try   4 have   5 learn   6 stay   7 visit

Grammar – Past continuous

4 Encourage the students to look at the picture and to tell you what the people are doing before they read the text.

> **Answers**
>
> 1 B   2 A   3 C

5 Ask the students if the activities in the text are happening now (present), later (future) or before (in the past). Check that the students can identify the past continuous. Encourage the students to say how we form the past continuous positive, negative, question and short answer. Point out that the spelling rules of the *–ing* form are the same as for the present continuous. If necessary, refer the students to the Grammar reference on page 85.

> **Answers**
>
> Students should underline: it <u>wasn't raining</u>, Dad <u>was building</u> a fire, my sister <u>was reading</u>, Kevin and I <u>were climbing</u> a tree.
>
> 1 Yesterday at 7 p.m.   2 No   3 No

6 With a stronger class, read the email to the class but stop before each verb to see if the students can provide the answer, e.g. *At 11 o'clock, the sun* [pause]

> **Answers**
>
> 1 was   2 wasn't   3 were   4 was   5 were   6 were

Further practice

The students write a reply to Kylie's email answering the question *What were you doing at 11 o'clock yesterday?*

> See the Workbook and CD ROM for further practice on Grammar & Vocabulary.

Listening

Part 2

1 Encourage students to tell you what they can remember about Listening Part 2 – they can look at the Exam task to help.

> **Answers**
>
> 1 Bella's talking to her dad about her friends and where they stayed on holiday.
> 2 Ivan
> 3 a campsite

2 Read the Exam task as a class. Remind the students that they may not hear the same word in the recording, it may be another word with a similar meaning.

> **Answers**
>
> 1 b   2 e   3 a   4 c   5 d

3 🔊 27 Point out that although the students will hear the words a–e on the recording, they should write one of the words 1–5 next to each name.

> **Answers**
>
> 1 2 clothes (a sweater)   2 3 a book (a dictionary)   3 5 a mobile (a phone)

> **Recording script**
>
> Sister: What are you doing Taylor?
> Taylor: I'm reading a message from Guy.
> Sister: Guy? Where is he?
> Taylor: He isn't having good time on holiday. He says the music in the disco is terrible and (1) <u>he forgot to pack his sweater</u> and it's really cold at night.
> Sister: Oh, no! Can't he borrow one from his brother?

Taylor:	From Matt? He's in Italy learning Italian. And (2) <u>Matt forgot to take his Italian dictionary</u> so he had to buy a new one and it cost £20!
Sister:	Really! What a family!
Taylor:	That's nothing. Did you hear about Naomi? She's also in Italy.
Sister:	No, what did she do?
Taylor:	(3) <u>She left her phone at home</u>. When she got to the airport, the Italian family wasn't waiting for her. She didn't have their phone number because her address book is on the phone.
Sister:	What did she do?
Taylor:	Well, she found the information desk and they phoned her mum and her mum ...

Exam task

🔊 28 Remind the students that they will hear the friends 0–5 in order. Encourage them to think of the words they might hear for each of the places A–H before they listen, e.g. A a farm, animals; B old, history; C sea, sail; D tent, countryside; E small, comfortable; F home, family; G flat; H small hotel. Play the recording twice.

Answers

1 G   2 E   3 B   4 F   5 H

Recording script

Listen to Bella talking to her dad about her friends.
Where did her friends stay on holiday?
For questions 1–5, write a letter A–H next to each friend.

Dad:	Bella, I've got a week's holiday in July. Why don't we go to the countryside and take the tent?
Bella:	Oh, no! (0) <u>My friend Ivan slept in a tent</u> last July and it rained all week.
Dad:	But I like the rain.
Bella:	Dad! (1) <u>Alfie went to Edinburgh in Scotland last year. They rented a flat</u> in the city centre. He said Edinburgh Castle was amazing.
Dad:	No, you know I don't really like cities.
Bella:	I was talking to (2) <u>Erica yesterday. She said they stayed in a small family hotel</u> in a little village in France. It was just like home! Why don't we go there?
Dad:	I'm not sure. What about your friend, Tanya? What did she do?
Bella:	Oh, yeah! (3) <u>She stayed with her family in a castle</u> on Malta. They drove to Italy and took a boat to Malta from there.
Dad:	That's sounds like a lot of driving! Any other ideas?
Bella:	Well, my friend Steven went to Thailand with his dad. They were looking for a hotel when (4) <u>a friend of his dad invited them to stay in his house</u>.
Dad:	Yes, but we've only got a week and Thailand is too far.
Bella:	I know! (5) <u>Lynne's family stayed near Stanton's Farm in a guest-house</u>. We could take our bikes and go cycling.
Dad:	Now that's a good idea.

4 With a weaker class, make the questions together and write them on the board first.

Suggested answers

How often do you visit capital cities? I love visiting capital cities. My favourite city is Paris.
Do you like learning the language? No, not really. My parents often speak English.
Do you like staying in a comfortable hotel? Of course, I do!
Do you often try new dishes? Yes, I do. I love trying new food.
Do you like having a rest? No, I prefer doing activities.
Do you like exploring somewhere new? Yes, I do. I like seeing new places and finding out about them.

Reading

Part 4

1 Ask the students to read the Exam task instructions and say what they have to do. Ask what the article is about. Then ask them to look again at the Reading Part 4 task in Unit 4 and to say how it differs from the task in this one. In Unit 4, you choose 'right', 'wrong' or 'doesn't say'. In this unit, you need to choose the correct answers A, B or C. Point out that the most common task type is as Unit 4. Read the Exam tip as a class. Discuss the answer to the example question after the students have underlined the words in the article.

Answers

Suggested words to underline: <u>I was doing my homework.</u>
B: the phone rang, Bethany didn't phone
C: her family were watching TV

Exam task

Encourage students to read the complete text to get a general idea before they start answering the questions. Remind them to underline the information in the text which gives them the answer to each question. When they have finished, encourage the students to compare their answers in pairs and to say why the other two answers are incorrect.

Answers

1 C (The next day, on my way home from school, I borrowed a guidebook from the library and then ...)
2 C (my dad drove me)
3 B (the sun was shining in Pointe-à-Pitre)
4 A (French is the language in Guadaloupe but none of us could speak it.)
5 C (After lunch, we visited different places in the city)
6 A (For the next two weeks, I stayed with the Dinart family in their house)
7 B (I liked walking up La Soufrière volcano best of all)

Further practice

In small groups, the students ask and answer questions about an amazing holiday. This can be a real holiday or a dream holiday. If necessary, help the students with the questions, e.g. *Where did you go? When did you go? Where did you stay? What did you do there?*

Grammar & vocabulary

Vocabulary – Adjectives of opinion

1 After completing the exercise, ask students to underline the adjectives in each of the sentences.

Answers
1 ✓ 2 ✗ 3 ✓ 4 ✗ 5 ✓ 6 ✗ 7 ✓

2 Encourage students to think about sentences they could use these adjectives in and complete the exercise. Students can then write a new sentence for some of these adjectives in pairs, e.g. *We had a great time at the party. It was brilliant.*

Answers
Good: brilliant, wonderful, amazing, interesting, exciting, funny, excellent
Bad: terrible, tiring, boring

3 If appropriate, highlight the difference between adjectives ending in *-ed* and *-ing*, e.g. *I was very excited* (someone feels: adjective + *-ed*) *because my holiday was exciting* (something is: adjective + *-ing*). Also point out that if we enjoy something, it is *fun* but something that makes you laugh is *funny*.

Answers
2 My holiday was so ~~excited~~ = exciting   3 it was very ~~bored~~ = boring   4 It was really exciting and ~~funny~~ = fun   5 This is a ~~beautifull~~ country = beautiful   6 we played a lot of ~~funy~~ games = funny

Further practice
Write these questions on the board: *What was your last birthday like? What was your last school trip like? What was your last exam like? What was the last film you saw like?* In pairs, the students take turns to ask these questions and answer them using the adjectives of opinion.

Grammar – Past simple & past continuous

4 Check that the students can identify the past simple and past continuous first. Elicit the rules for when we use the past simple and past continuous from the class by asking these questions: *Do we use the past simple or continuous when we describe activities happening at a moment and we're not interested when the activity started or finished?* (past continuous) *Do we use the past simple or continuous to talk about complete actions?* (past simple) *When do we use the past simple and continuous together?* (When we want to say an action happened in the middle of an activity) With a weaker class, it may be necessary to guide the students to these answers using the question, e.g. *Look at the first example. Do we know when I started my homework?* (No) *Are we interested?* (No) *In the second sentence, did I get to the internet café?* (Yes, it's a complete action) *In the third sentence, what happened first?* (raining) *When did I leave Ireland?* (in the middle of the rain).

Answers
Underline: borrowed, went, left
Circle: was doing, were watching, was raining

5 Make sure that the students spell the past simple and the *-ing* form correctly. If necessary, refer them to the spelling rules in the Grammar reference on page 85. Then ask the students to underline the examples of *when* and circle the examples of *while*. Ask them to say whether we usually use the past simple or past continuous after *while* (past continuous).

Answers
1 started   2 was packing   3 was studying   4 tried
5 was swimming   6 were visiting

6 Point out that the students need to complete the questions in the past simple or past continuous. Then, in pairs, the students take turns to ask and answer the questions.

Suggested answers
1 Was it raining when you woke up this morning? No, it wasn't. The sun was shining.
2 What were you doing when the teacher came in? I was talking to my friends.
3 What did you watch on TV while you were having dinner yesterday? I didn't watch TV while I was having dinner.
4 Was your mum watching TV when you got home? No, she wasn't. She was reading a newspaper.

> See the Workbook and CD ROM for further practice on Grammar & Vocabulary.

Writing

Part 8

1 Invite a brief class discussion on whether the students have ever bought a present for their teacher. Encourage them to say when, why and what they bought.

Answer
A DVD

2 Encourage the students to read Martina's notes carefully first and to say what type of information is missing, i.e. 1 name 2 day of the week 3 time 4 £ price 5 a telephone number. Point out that the words in the notes may not be the same as the words in the answers.

Answers
2 Monday   3 5   4 £13.99   5 876234

Exam task
Encourage the students to read the Exam task instructions and to say what they have to do. (Read an advertisement and an email and complete Jared's notes). Read the Exam tip as a class and point out that in Exercise 2, there were two possible answers but only one was correct. Ask the students to read Carolina's note first and to say what she wants to buy for her teacher (a guidebook). Then, encourage the students to read Jared's notes carefully first and to say what type of information is missing in each space (1–5).

Answers

1 My Africa   2 Tuesday   3 567342   4 9   5 10

Speaking

Part 2

1 🔘 29 Encourage the students to look at the information about the holiday first and to say whether they would like to go on this holiday before they listen. Point out that question 4 on this page asks for a price in dollars ($), however in the exam all the prices are in pounds (£). With a stronger class, ask the student to write the complete questions before they listen and then to listen and check their answers.

Answers

2 Is it open in the summer?
3 What can I do there?
4 How much is it?
5 How can I get more information?

Recording script

Johannes:	(1) Where is it, Eva?
Eva:	It's in Lake City in California.
Johannes:	(2) Is it open in the summer?
Eva:	It's open from 1st May to 7th September.
Johannes:	(3) What can I do there?
Eva:	You can see some of the tallest trees in the world.
Johannes:	That sounds amazing. (4) How much is it?
Eva:	It's only $35 per car and $5 per person.
Johannes:	Cool! (5) How can I get more information?
Eva:	Look at their website. It's www.AmericaHoliday.com

---

2 Read the Exam tip as a class. Ask the students if Eva answered the questions well and why. (She answers them well because she uses complete sentences.) Then students take turns to ask and answer the questions about Yellow Creek Campsite in pairs.

Answers

2 It's open from   3 You can   4 It's   5 Look at their website. It's

Exam task

Read the complete instructions to the students:

Student A, here is some information about a holiday. Student B, you don't know anything about the holiday, so ask student A some questions about it. Now, student B, ask student A your questions about the holiday, and student A, you answer them.

Holiday on the Nile, Egypt
Alexandria Boat Hotel

November 1st to April 30th

Explore the river and learn about history

£100 for a family room

www.EgyptBoats.com

Holiday on the Nile, Egypt

♦ name / hotel ?

♦ when / stay ?

♦ what / do ?

♦ cost? £ ?

♦ website ?

Student B, here is some information about a new travel programme for young people. Student A, you don't know anything about the travel programme so ask student B some questions about it. Now student A, ask student B your questions and student B, you answer them.

New Travel Programme
'Amazing Adventures'

Watch young travellers explore the world

Mondays & Thursdays

7.30 p.m. – 8.00 p.m.

Find out more on the Channel 7 website

New Travel Programme

♦ what / name ?

♦ what / see ?

♦ start ? 🕐

♦ on every day ?

♦ more information ?

Remind students to ask complete questions and answer in full sentences. If they don't understand a question, they can use *Sorry?* or *Can you repeat that, please?*

Suggested answers

B: What's the name of the hotel? / What's the hotel's name?
A: It's the Alexandria Boat Hotel.
B: When can I stay there?
A: You can stay there from November 1st to April 30th.
B: What can I do there?
A: You can explore the river and learn about history.
B: How much is it?
A: It's £100 for a family room.
B: Is there a website?
A: Yes, it's www.EgyptBoats.com.

A: What's the name (of the new travel programme)?
B: It's Amazing Adventures.
A: What can I see?
B: You can watch young travellers explore the world.
A: What time does it start?
B: It starts at 7.30 p.m.
A: Is it on every day?
B: No, it's on Mondays and Thursdays.
A: How can I get more information?
B: You can find out more on the Channel 7 website.

⭐ **CLIL** History (Ancient Civilisations): In small groups, students choose an Ancient Civilisation (e.g. Egypt, China, Greece, etc.) and look on the Internet for some information on cities, transport, clothes, food and drink, etc. Each group produces a poster display with the information. The British Museum website has some interesting web links for students (http://tinyurl.com/ycb8xfc).

9

What's on?

Unit objectives

KEY FOR SCHOOLS TOPICS	entertainment & media, television
GRAMMAR	*be going to*, infinitives & *-ing* forms
VOCABULARY	entertainment, television, word-building
READING	Part 3b: Understanding suggestions and answering them correctly
WRITING	Part 9: Using *and*, *or*, *but* and *because* to improve writing
LISTENING	Part 4: Writing one answer only
SPEAKING	Part 1: Answering questions about future plans

Entertainment & media

Reading

Part 3b

Vocabulary – Going out

1 With books closed, brainstorm a list of types of entertainment, e.g. concert, circus, film, play, etc. Invite a brief class discussion on what people can see in the students' town and where they can find information about what's on. With books open, point out that this is a programme from an arts centre.

> **Answers**
>
> 2 film   3 dance   4 circus   5 exhibition

Further practice
In pairs, students talk about the things they'd like to see, e.g. *Would you like to see the film? No thanks! I don't like adventure films. Would you like to see the dance competition? Yes, because I love dancing.* etc.

2 (○━ 30) Point out that Aidan and Aysha decide to see one of the events in Exercise 1.

> **Answer**
>
> The circus

> **Recording script**
>
> Aidan: Let's go to the Centre this weekend.
>
> Aysha: That's a good idea. What's on?
>
> Aidan: Look at this programme! There's a new adventure film on at 4.00 on Saturday.
>
> Aysha: Oh, no thanks. I saw it last week.
>
> Aidan: What about the dance competition at 6 o'clock?
>
> Aysha: I'm not sure. Why don't we go to the concert on Friday night?
>
> Aidan: I'm sorry, I can't. I'm going to have dinner with my cousins on Friday.

> Aysha: Are you free on Sunday? <u>How about the circus?</u>
>
> Aidan: <u>Great!</u> Shall we meet at the bus stop at 2 o'clock?
>
> Aysha: Brilliant. See you there.

3 Encourage the students to read the complete conversation first and think about what Aysha said before they look at the expressions a–e and start writing.

> **Answers**
>
> 2 c   3 e   4 d   5 a

4 Ask the students to look at the Exam task and to say what they have to do in this part. Read the Exam tip as a class.

> **Answers**
>
> | Suggestions | Answers | |
> | --- | --- | --- |
> | | ✓ | X |
> | What about the dance competition? | | I'm not sure. |
> | Why don't we go to the concert? | | I'm sorry, I can't. |
> | How about the circus? | Great! | |
> | Shall we meet at the bus stop? | Brilliant! | |

5 Remind the students to read the part given (A or B) carefully as this will help them find the answer, e.g. 1 A asks about the '<u>cinema</u>' and the answer B is 'I don't like <u>films</u>'. Encourage the students to think about a possible answer before they look at the expressions a–e. As you are checking the answers, ask the students to say which words helped them find the answers: 2 A outside the theatre – B there 3 A circus – B clowns 4 A on Sunday – B at the weekend 5 A watch TV – B Channel 3

> **Answers**
>
> 2 c   3 d   4 b   5 a

Exam task

Encourage the students to read the complete task without writing first and to say what information they find out, e.g. Robbie would like to go to the cinema with Ashley on Saturday afternoon; they're going to see a Japanese cartoon; Robbie's staying with his aunt, etc. Remind the students to read the information before and after the space before they choose the correct answer. They should also cross out the answer when they find it. Encourage the students to compare their answers and to say why their answer is correct, e.g. *In (1), I put G because Ashley says yes to the suggestion and then asks 'What's on?' Robbie then answers this question with 'A new film about ...'.*

> **Answers**
>
> 1 G   2 E   3 D   4 A   5 B

Grammar – *be going to*: positive and negative

6 With books closed, ask questions 1–3 around the class to see how much the students remember. With books open, the students check their ideas and answer question 4.

Answers

1 On Saturday afternoon.   2 Because Robbie's going to stay at his aunt's house.   3 No, he doesn't.   4 *be going to* + infinitive.

7 Refer the students to the Grammar reference on page 86 and highlight the form of *be going to*: positive and negative before they do this exercise. Encourage the students to read the text first and answer the question *What is Madison going to do in the summer holidays*? before writing.

Answers

2 isn't (is not) going to meet   3 's (is) going to join 4 're (are) going to spend   5 're (are) going to do   6 're (are) going to have   7 isn't (is not) going to be   8 'm (am) not going to see 9 're (are) going to watch

Further practice

Students write a new conversation between two friends using suggestions and *going to*. Students can use the Exam task conversation to help them.

> See the Workbook and CD ROM for further practice on Grammar & Vocabulary.

Listening

Part 4

1 If appropriate, ask the students to translate this word into their own language.

Suggested answer

worried and nervous

2 Invite a brief class discussion on whether there are reality shows where people perform short acts in their countries. Popular shows in the UK include *The X Factor* and *Britain's Got Talent*. Encourage the students to use *be going to* in their answers.

Suggested answer

2 They're going to dance.   3 Her dog's going to jump.   4 He's going to do a play.   5 They're going to do street dancing.

3 ◄— 31 Encourage the students to look at the Exam task and to say what they have to do in this part (complete some notes) and how many people they listen to (two: Syed and Katia). Read the Exam task as a class and point out that this Exam tip is in fact true for all the parts of the exam. Point out that the students may hear both answers, only one is correct. Discuss with the students what the other answer refers to.

Answers

1 Teen week   2 TV   3 guitar   4 5   5 sports centre

Recording script

Katia:	Hi, Syed! Syed!
Syed:	Oh hi, Katia!
Katia:	Are you reading *Sports Today* magazine again?
Syed:	No, (1) <u>I'm reading *Teen Week*. Look at this advertisement!</u>
Katia:	What's it for?
Syed:	Well, you know we did an audition last year for the school show? (2) <u>Well, this is an audition for a TV show.</u> Shall we do it?
Katia:	Yes, it was fun but I'm not sure.
Syed:	Come on! We did really well last year. (3) <u>Why don't you play the guitar</u> and I'll play the violin?
Katia:	Oh, all right. What do we need to do next? Do we have to send an email?
Syed:	Yes, I'll send the email but we also need to practise.
Katia:	Let's start tomorrow at two o'clock.
Syed:	I'm sorry, I can't. (4) <u>Can we meet later at five?</u>
Katia:	Great. Where can we practise? The music school is closed tomorrow.
Syed:	Don't worry. (5) <u>We can practise at the sports centre.</u>
Katia:	Cool! See you tomorrow then.

Exam task

◄— 32 Encourage the students to read the notes and to say what sort of information is missing before they listen, e.g. 1 a time in the afternoon; 2 transport; 3 place; 4 an object; 5 name. Remind the students that they may hear two possible answers but only one is correct and they should write down one answer only. Point out that the spelling of the name must be correct. Play the recording twice. During the feedback stage, check that the students have spelt the name correctly.

Answers

1 6.30 / half past six   2 car   3 school   4 a snack   5 Hollard

---

Recording script

You will hear a boy, Syed, talking to Katia about an audition for a TV show.

Listen and complete each question.

Syed:	Hi, Katia!
Katia:	Hi, Syed!
Syed:	I've got all the information about the audition for the TV show.
Katia:	Cool!
Syed:	(0) <u>It's going to be on Wednesday</u> 14th.
Katia:	I hope that's after lessons. You know we shouldn't miss any.
Syed:	No. It's fine. Lessons finish at four and (1) <u>the audition is at half past six</u>, so it'll be fine.
Katia:	OK. How are we going to get there? The bus is so slow.

Syed:	Don't worry. (2) <u>My mum's going to take us in her car</u>. She has to come with us anyway because we're under 18.
Katia:	Great! Is she going to collect me from my flat?
Syed:	(3) <u>She'll come to school</u> and take us from there.
Katia:	OK. Do we have to take anything special?
Syed:	We can't take photos so don't bring your camera (4) <u>but don't forget a snack</u>. We may be there for hours.
Katia:	And where do we go when we get there?
Syed:	When we get there, we have to ask for the TV show receptionist. Her name is … is … I wrote her name here. Yes, (5) <u>it's Paula Hollard. That's H-O-double L-A-R-D</u>.
Katia:	I'm really excited, Syed.
Syed:	Me, too.

Further practice

In small groups, students imagine they are going to do an audition for the music show on TV. They should talk together about what the group is going to do (sing, dance, act, etc.), what each member is going to do (play an instrument, write the play, etc.), what they are going to wear. When they are ready, each group tells the class what they are going to do, e.g. *Our group is going to do a pop song. I'm going to sing, Ana is going to play the guitar and Francesca is going to play the drums. Freddie and Maria are going to dance.* Then the students vote for the best idea.

Television

Speaking

Part 1

Vocabulary – TV programmes

1 The TV programmes in this exercise are the ones that appear on the Key for Schools vocabulary list but brainstorm other types of TV programmes, e.g. Reality Shows, talent show, documentary, etc. This will help the students do Exercise 2.

Answers

2 the weather   3 the news   4 quiz show

2 Encourage the students to answer in full sentences giving reasons with *because*. Then ask students to give a brief report to the class about their partner's favourite TV programmes.

Suggested answers

1 I watch TV every day after dinner.
2 I like watching sports programmes because I love all kinds of sports.
3 I don't like watching cartoons because they are boring and they are for children.

3 Read the Exam tip as a class. Point out that all the questions in this exercise ask about future plans and highlight the question. If necessary, refer the students to the Grammar

reference on page 86. Also point out that the first word in each question begins with a capital letter.

Answers

2 What are you going to watch on TV later?
3 Are you going to see a film tomorrow?
4 What are you going to do at the weekend?
5 Are you going to do anything special on Saturday night?
6 What are your plans for next week?

4 Monitor as the students are asking and answering the questions. Make a note of any mistakes and go over these as a class when they have finished the activity. You could ask some pairs to ask and answer a question for the whole class.

5 ◖33◗ Point out that the examiner doesn't ask Ella and Emir the same question.

Answer

Ella: 4   Emir: 6

Recording script

Examiner:	Now Ella, (1) <u>what are you going to do at the weekend</u>?
Ella:	With friends.
Examiner:	Thank-you. Emir, (2) <u>what are your plans for next week</u>?
Emir:	I'm going to go to school of course. I'm also going to see a film at the cinema with my friends.

6 A stronger class might be able to answer this without listening again. Students should justify their answers.

Answers

Emir because he answers the examiner's question in full sentences with *going to*.

Exam task

Ask the students to take turns to be the examiner and candidate. Remind the candidate to answer in a complete sentence with the correct form of *be going to*.

Suggested answers

What are you going to do this evening? After this class, I'm going to walk home. I'm going to do my homework and watch TV.

What are your plans for the next school holidays? I think I'm going to stay at my grandparents' house.

Grammar & vocabulary

Grammar – Infinitives & -ing forms

1 Encourage the students to look at the photo and to say what they can see. It is a photo of the WOMAD festival which is an international arts festival. Ask the students if there is a WOMAD festival in their country.

Background information (see http://womad.org)

There are WOMADs in over 27 countries. There is a five minute video on youtube introducing this festival (http://www.youtube.com/watch?v=5WpSafFS6PI).

Answer

The Kodo Drummers from Japan, the National Dance Company of Cambodia and a jazz band from India.

2 Refer the students to the Grammar reference on page 86 and ask the students to say when we use an infinitive (after some verbs and after an adjective) and an -ing form (after some verbs and after a preposition). Point out that students will have to learn which verbs are followed by an infinitive and which are followed by an -ing form. Encourage the students to underline the main verbs in the sentences (e.g. sentence 1 = would like) and then elicit the correct form of the following verb.

Answers

2 decided to ~~bought~~ = to buy   3 interested in ~~learn~~ = learning   4 I hope ~~hearing~~ = to hear   5 easy ~~find~~ = to find   6 How about ~~to go~~ = going

3 Encourage the students to read the complete email first before they start writing.

Answers

1 watching   2 listening   3 to see   4 to buy   5 to show   6 to hear

Vocabulary – Word-building

4 Remind the students of the spelling rules, i.e. double the letter and add -er when it's a short rather than long vowel sound, e.g. mm in drummer; -r for words ending in -er e.g. dancer; add -er for words ending in other letters.

Answers

2 writer   3 dancer   4 photographer   5 singer   6 painter

5 Remind the students to count the spaces as these tell them how many letters are missing.

Answers

1 artist   2 musician   3 actor   4 guitarist   5 journalist

Further practice

Students talk together about the things they'd like to see at an Arts festival. They could write a message for a class blog, e.g. *I'd like to listen to cool music and see my favourite musicians. I hope to see something new and exciting, for example, I love watching dancers from other countries.*

CLIL Music: In small groups, students find some information about a type of music, e.g. jazz, classical, opera, folk, rap, etc. Each group produces a short presentation with information about famous musicians, instruments, concerts and a short sound or video clip to illustrate their chosen type of music.

See the Workbook and CD ROM for further practice on Grammar & Vocabulary.

Writing

Part 9

1 Invite a brief class discussion on what the students have to do in this part. If necessary, ask the students to look at the Exam task first. Read the Exam tip as a class.

Answers

1 b   2 c   3 d   4 e   5 a

2 First check that the students have understood what each connector means by asking them to say which word says why / gives a reason (*because*), which word adds more information (*and*), which word shows two or more possibilities (*or*) and which word introduces a contrast (*but*).

Answers

2 We're not going to the dance festival because there aren't any tickets left.
3 We can see a play or we can see a film.
4 Don't forget to see the Drummers of Burundi and don't forget to bring your camera.
5 I don't like acting in plays but I like watching them.

3 Read the Exam task as a class and ask the students to say who they need to write to (a friend) and how many pieces of information they need to include (three). Read the student's answer and point out that if the marker can't read a student's answer, he or she won't be able to give a mark.

Answers

The teacher asked Aleksy to rewrite his answer.

4 As a follow-up, the students say how many marks (out of five) they think Aleksy's answer will get. The students should justify their answer. Point out that Aleksy's answer is now a model answer and gets full marks; it starts and finishes well, it includes all three pieces of information and it is 35 words.

Answers

2 or   3 but

5 Brainstorm a list of possible shows as a class first. Remind students to use *and*, *but*, *because* and *or* in their answers.

Model answer

Hi
I'm going to see the Beijing Circus on Saturday. Would you like to come? We can go at five or seven. We could walk there but let's go by bus.
Bye for now,

6 Remind the students to leave time in the exam to check their work. Students can often learn a lot from reading each other's work. If appropriate, encourage the students to read each other's Exam task and to use the writing checklist to say if it is a good answer.

10

Are you an outdoors person?

Unit objectives

KEY FOR SCHOOLS TOPICS	the natural world, weather
GRAMMAR	*will / won't* and *may*, first conditional
VOCABULARY	places in the countryside, prepositions of place, weather
READING	Part 1: Looking for words with a similar meaning (*not* + adjective)
WRITING	Part 8: Checking spelling
LISTENING	Part 1: Deciding where things are
SPEAKING	Part 2: Using expressions like *Oh!*, *Great!* & *Thanks!* to show interest

The natural world

Listening

Part 1

Vocabulary – The countryside

1 Encourage the students to look at the map and identify the places A–H before they look at the words.

> **Answers**
>
> 2 river F   3 gate B   4 path D   5 hill H   6 field C   7 wood E
> 8 farm A

2 Point out that the students need to look at the map in Exercise 1 as they follow the instructions. Encourage the students to draw Ned's route with a pencil.

> **Answers**
>
> Put a cross (X) under the first picnic table (on the left).

3 Read the Exam tip as a class and point out that the students will often hear prepositions of place, e.g. *behind, under, in, on,* etc. Ask the students to read through Ned's instructions in Exercise 2 again and underline the prepositions of place. Encourage the students to say where George's ball is using the preposition.

> **Answers**
>
> A: It's in a tree.   B: It's under the table.   C: It's behind the gate.

4 🔘 34 Play the recording twice so that the students can listen for the words. Ask the students to say what the other two pictures refer to. (The ball was under the table; Tom threw it behind the gate).

> **Answers**
>
> Mum says: Look it's there, in the tree.

Recording script

Where is George's ball?

George: I can't find the ball.

Mum: It was under the table a minute ago.

George: Yes, and then Tom threw it behind that gate.

Mum: (0) <u>Look it's there, in the tree</u>. Why is it there, George?

The answer is A.

Exam task

🔘 35 Encourage the students to look at each set of pictures and to describe what they can see in each and if appropriate, say where things are. Point out that the students will hear each recording twice. Encourage the students to compare their answers in pairs and to say what the other two pictures refer to.

> **Answers**
>
> 1 B   2 C   3 B   4 A   5 C

Recording script

You will hear five short conversations.

You will hear each conversation twice.

There is one question for each conversation.

For each question, choose the right answer (A, B or C).

Look at question 1

1 Where will Joel and his family stay this year?

Joel: Dad, can we go to that hotel next to the river again this year?

Dad: Sorry, Joel. Your mother didn't like it very much.

Joel: How about that place on top of that hill? We stayed there two years ago.

Dad: That's full so Mum and <u>I found one in Great Woods. I booked it last night</u>.

Now listen again.

2 How much do Daniella's walking boots cost on the website?

Daniella: I saw some great new walking boots in town today but they were £120.

Mum: Why don't you look online? Your cousin bought some boots for £100.

Daniella: <u>I looked at www.bestboots.com and the cheapest ones were £130.</u>

Mum: Oh really? Let's go and buy them in the shop in town then.

Now listen again.

3 What time does the park close today?

Girl: Excuse me. What time is it?

Man: It's five thirty.

Girl: Really? Does the park close at half past six?

| Man: | It's Sunday today, so <u>it shuts at six</u> – it stays open later on Saturdays. |

Now listen again.

4 What will they do in the afternoon?

Girl:	That was great! I love windsurfing on this lake.
Boy:	Yes, it was. What's next?
Girl:	<u>After lunch we're going to build a tree house.</u>
Boy:	Cool! And tomorrow we're going mountain biking. I love being outdoors.

Now listen again.

5 Where are dad's keys?

Dad:	I can't find my car keys. I thought I left them on that bag.
Girl:	Look on the floor. Maybe you dropped them.
Dad:	They're not here. <u>I think they may still be inside the car.</u>
Girl:	I'll look ... <u>You're right, Dad, here they are!</u>

Now listen again.

Grammar – *will / won't* and *may*

5 Ask students if the sentences are referring to the present, past or future (Answer: future). Check students understand *certain, possible, impossible* before they do the exercise.

Answers
1 b 2 c 3 a

6 Highlight the form of *will* and *may*. Point out that the negative of *will* is *won't* and the question form is *Will you ...?* Also point out that *will* and *may* are the same for all persons (*I, you, he ...*) and after these words, we use the infinitive without *to*. If necessary, refer the students to the Grammar reference on page 87.

Answers
2 I ~~wait~~ = 'll (will) wait   3 ~~not will~~ = won't (will not) be   4 ~~maybe~~ = may wear   5 we ~~take~~ = 'll (will) take   6 ~~maybe~~ = may be   7 ~~wont~~ = won't (will not) rain   8 I ~~see~~ = I'll (will) see

7 Encourage the students to read the complete conversation before they start writing. Ask fast finishers to continue the conversation using *will / won't* and *may*.

Answers
2 may rain   3 will you get   4 may go   5 may drive   6 'll (will) take   7 won't be   8 'll (will) have

> See the Workbook and CD ROM for further practice on Grammar & Vocabulary.

Weather

Reading

Part 1

Vocabulary – Weather & seasons

1 With books closed, invite a brief discussion on the weather, e.g. *What's the weather like today? What was the weather like yesterday? What will the weather be like tomorrow?* After completing the exercise, ask students to make adjectives for the weather nouns (all except thunderstorm): *icy, cloudy, foggy, rainy, snowy, stormy, sunny, windy.*

Answers
2 wind   3 rain   4 fog   5 cloud   6 thunderstorm

2 If necessary, point out that seasons are very different all over the world. This will depend on the hemisphere and also how close to the Equator the country is. Invite a brief class discussion on which of the places in this exercise the students would like to visit.

Answers
2 winter   3 autumn   4 spring

Further practice
In small groups, students discuss the question *When is the best time to visit your country?* They choose a reporter from the group who gives the rest of the class their group's opinion and reasons.

CLIL Geography / Maths: In small groups, students choose a city from a very different part of the world and write a short answer for the website question: *When is the best time to visit your city?* The students should find information about the city's weather and seasons and present this information using a weather map, a temperature bar chart and rainfall graph. Encourage the students to calculate the average rainfall and average temperatures per month, season and year. The group's answer should include a map to show where it is, a photo of the place and the information about the weather. As a class, read all the answers and vote on the best place to visit in winter, spring, summer and autumn. The KidsGo website (http://kidsgotravelguides.com/) has travel information for young people, including information about the weather.

3 Book closed. Encourage the students to close their eyes and imagine they're in a large park in the countryside. It's a beautiful summer's day. Ask the students to say what they can see (children playing, a lot of trees, grass, etc.). Then ask them to say if they can see any notices and elicit what is on them.

Suggested answers
No cycling, Don't walk on the grass, Don't climb the trees, etc.

4 Encourage the students to look at the Exam task and to say what they have to do in this part. (Match some sentences with the correct notice.)

5 Read the Exam tip as a class first. Remind the students to look for *not* + opposites in this exercise.

> **Answers**
> 2 open   3 running   4 over   5 dry   6 easy

Exam task

Remind the students that they won't find exactly the same words in the notices. They should look for words with a similar meaning. Also remind the students to cross out the answer as they find it.

> **Answers**
> 1 E   2 C   3 A   4 F   5 G

Further practice

In pairs, students choose a new place, e.g. a museum, an airport, a sports centre, a town centre, a festival, etc. and write three notices. Then in small groups, they take turns to read out their three notices. The other members of the group try to guess where they can see these notices, e.g.

A: *Our notices are No food or drink, No photography and Free entrance on Mondays 5–7p.m.*

B: *Can you see them in a museum?*

Grammar – First conditional

6 Ask the students to look at the cartoon and to say what they can see first, i.e. countryside, field, gate, notice, cow, farmer, etc.

> **Answers**
> 1 No, it's closed.   2 Inside the field.   3 No, because the gate is closed and the cows are in the field but if someone opens the gate and the cows run away, he'll be angry.

7 Focus the students' attention on the two sentences in Exercise 6 and highlight the form and use of the first conditional: *If* +present simple (possible situation), *will/won't* + infinitive (possible result) (or *will/won't* + infinitive *if* + present simple). If necessary, refer the students to the Grammar reference on page 87. Remind students that *will* and *won't* are always followed by the infinitive without *to*. Point out that we use a comma ',' in the girl's sentence *If the gate's open, …* because this sentence begins with *If*. The boy's sentence *And the farmer won't be pleased …* begins with the result, so we don't use a comma ','. Encourage the students to read the complete conversation before they start writing. Ask fast finishers to continue the conversation using the first conditional.

> **Answers**
> 2 won't (will not) get   3 'll (will) find   4 'll (will) we do   5 find
> 6 find   7 won't (will not) stay   8 get   9 'll (will) phone
> 10 get   11 doesn't (does not) answer   12 'll (will) call

> See the Workbook and CD ROM for further practice on Grammar & Vocabulary.

Writing

Part 8

1 Ask the students to look at the Exam task and to say what they have to do in this part: read the notice and the email and complete Lisa's trip booking form. The students are asked to read the Exam task more carefully in Exercise 2. Read the Exam tip as a class and point out that as they will be copying words from the information given in this part, they can't make mistakes with spelling.

> **Answers**
> 2 volleyball   3 tennis competition   4 tomorrow   5 camera

2 Point out that the students shouldn't complete the form now; they should just answer the question.

> **Answer**
> Lisa wants Vicki to complete her trip form because she can't go to the meeting.

Exam task

Remind the students to look at the form first and think about what sort of words are missing in each answer. Also remind the students to check their spelling before they finish.

> **Answer**
> 1 Great Canal   2 3–4 July   3 607901   4 train   5 tent

Further practice

In pairs, students write an email to a friend inviting them to go on the trip, too. They should include information about when they're going, what they'll see and what their friend needs to bring.

Speaking

Part 2

1 First invite a brief class discussion on whether the students would like to go on the trip. Then give them time to write questions in pairs.

> **Suggested answers**
> 2 What can I / you do there?
> 3 How much does it cost?
> 4 Is it for teenagers?
> 5 When is it?
> 6 How can I get more information? / Is there a website?

2 🔘 36 Point out that the students will listen to two English-speaking friends and not two exam candidates. Play the recording twice if necessary.

> **Answers**
> Rachel's questions
> 1 Where is it?
> 2 What can you do there?
> 3 How much does it cost?
> 4 Is it for young people?
> 5 When can we do it?
> 6 How can we get more information? Have they got a website?

3 Read the Exam tip as a class. Encourage the students to think about the missing words in the exercise before they listen again. As a follow-up, in pairs, students take turns to ask and answer the questions about the Adventure Weekend in Exercise 1. They should try to use the expressions in this exercise to show they're interested.

Answers

2 Oh!   2 Cool!   3 Great!   4 OK   5 Sounds good.   6 Thanks

Exam task

Read the complete examiner's instructions to the class.

Student A, here is some information about a camping trip. Student B, you don't know anything about the camping trip, so ask A some questions about it. Use these words to help you. Now, student B, ask your questions about the camping group, and student A, you answer them.

Camping trip	Camping trip
for anyone 11 – 15 years old North Lake Campsite Saturday 14th and Sunday 15th May  Only £60 for the weekend Call Greg on 564899	♦ when ? ♦ cost ? £ ? ♦ where / stay ? ♦ more information ? ♦ for children ?

Student B, here is some information about an adventure park. Student A, you don't know anything about the adventure, so ask student B some questions about it. Use these words to help you. Now, student A, ask your questions about the adventure, and student B, you answer them.

Adventure Park	Adventure Park
 Jackson Wood April – September 10.00 a.m. – 5.00 p.m. Family ticket only £20 Call or text 560219	♦ where ?  ♦ open / all year ? ♦ expensive ? ♦ what time / open ? ♦ more information ?

Further practice

Students use the questions in the Exam task to ask and answer questions about their favourite shop in their town.

Remind students to ask complete questions, to answer in full sentences and to use some of the expressions in Exercise 3 to show they're interested in their partner's answer.

Suggested answers

B: When is it?
A: The next trip is 14th to 15th May.
B: Great! How much does it cost?
A: It's only £60 for the weekend.
B: Cool! Where will I stay?
A: You will stay at North Lake Campsite.
B: Sounds good! How can I get more information?
A: You can call Greg on 564899.
B: OK. Is it for children?
A: Yes, it's for anyone 11–15 years old.
B: Thanks.

A: Where is the Adventure Park?
B: It's in Jackson Wood.
A: Cool! Is it open all year?
B: No, it's open April to September.
A: Is it expensive?
B: No, a family ticket is only £20.
A: Great! What time does it open?
B: It opens at 10 a.m.
A: Sound good! How can I get more information? / Is there a telephone number?
B: Yes, it's 560219.
A: Thanks.

Further practice

In small groups, students make an advertisement for their own outdoors weekend. They can use the information about the Adventure Weekend in Exercise 1 and the Camping Group in Exercise 5 to help. They should say: where it is, what you can do there, how much it is, what ages it is for and how others can get more information (e.g. a website or email address or a phone number). The students should then change groups and take turns to ask and answer information about their outdoors weekends.

11 Healthy body, healthy mind

Unit objectives

Health & medicine

Reading

Part 5

Vocabulary – The body

1 With books closed, challenge the students to name as many parts of the body as they can. The students will then write down these words in Exercise 3. Pre-teach *grow, brush* and *sneeze* before the students do the quiz. Don't tell the students the answers for now. Ask them to read the text in Exercise 2 to find their answers.

> **Answers**
> 1 b 1.25cms a month   2 c 2 to 3 minutes

2 Encourage the students to underline the answers in the text. When the students have finished, ask them to tell you what other information they find out.

> **Answers**
> 1 Most people's hair grows 1.25 centimetres a month.
> 2 Brush them for two to three minutes at least twice a day.

3 Encourage the students to add more parts of the body to the table. Students won't be able to add *hair* because it's uncountable. If the students brainstormed some parts of the body in Exercise 1, they should also add these. Point out that the plural forms of *foot* and *tooth* are *feet* and *teeth*.

> **Answers**
>
> | one | two | more than two |
> | --- | --- | --- |
> | neck, stomach, back, nose, mouth | ear, eye, hand, leg, foot | tooth |

Grammar – Present perfect; *just*

4 Exercises 4 and 5 focus on the form of the present perfect. Make sure the students can recognise the present perfect before they look for examples in the text.

> **Answers**
> My mum has just cut my hair; I've just been to the dentist; And have you bought a new toothbrush this year?
> The past participle always comes after *have* or *has* in the present perfect.

5 Point out that some verbs are regular and the past participle form is verb + -*ed* (like the past simple) and other verbs are irregular. If necessary, refer the students to the spelling rules for regular verbs in the Grammar reference on page 88. There is an irregular verb table on page 96.

> **Answers**
> 2 My friends have ~~spended~~ = spent   3 We've ~~eatten~~ = eaten
> 4 We've ~~choosen~~ = chosen   5 I've ~~writed~~ = written
> 6 I've ~~forgetten~~ = forgotten

6 Encourage the students to look at the picture first and to say what has happened (*A boy has just fallen off his skateboard and he's hurt his leg. The girl has phoned for an ambulance.*). Ask the students to read what the girl says. Point out that we often use the present perfect to describe an action which happened before now (*I've phoned for an ambulance*) and we use *just* to say we did this a very short time ago. Point out that we use *just* between *have/has* and the past participle: *He's just cut his finger.*

> **Answers**
> 2 's (has) just cut   3 've (have) just had   4 've (have) just visited
> 5 've (have) just brushed   6 have just given

Grammar – *yet / already*

7 Focus attention on the 'To do' list. Explain that Ray and Sue are planning a party and the list includes what they have to do. The tick shows they have done that item. Students check the answers in pairs before you check as a class.

> **Answers**
> 2 ✓   3 ✗

8 Ask the students to say which two words mean *before now* (*already* and *yet*) in Exercise 7. Elicit that we normally use *already* for positive sentences and *yet* for negative sentences and questions. Explain *already* normally goes in the middle and *yet* at the end of the sentence. Encourage the students to read the complete email first before writing, Then they should write the correct form of the verb in the present perfect before they choose *yet* or *already*. Refer students to the Grammar reference on page 88.

> **Answers**
> 2 have just visited   3 has already made   4 Have you seen it yet?
> 5 haven't talked ... yet

9 Look at the Exam task together as a class and ask the students to say what they have to do in this part (read a text and choose the correct answer A, B or C). Then read the Exam tip as a class. Point out that in this exercise the verbs have two parts and the students have to choose the right form of either the first or second part.

> **Answers**
> 2 brushing   3 Did   4 climbing   5 have

Exam task

Encourage the students to read the complete article first without writing and to say what it is about.

> **Answers**
> 1 B   2 A   3 C   4 B   5 C   6 A   7 C   8 A

> **CLIL** Biology: In small groups, students choose another product related to health, for example, the toothbrush or toothpaste, the hearing aid, the walking stick, a hairbrush or soap. Encourage each group to choose something different. They should find some information on the Internet and write their own short history.

> See the Workbook and CD ROM for further practice on Grammar & Vocabulary.

Reading

Part 3a

Vocabulary – Health & illness

1 With books closed, brainstorm a list of problems associated with parts of the body, e.g. teeth (toothache), back (backache or my back hurts), head (headache or my head hurts), etc. Point out that with some words we say *I've got (a) back / head / tooth / stomach*, etc. *ache* and with others we say *My head / back / leg*, etc. *hurts*. Then encourage the students to think of some possible cures, e.g. *I've got a headache. – You should lie down.*, etc.

> **Answers**
> 2 c   3 f   4 e   5 a   6 b

2 Encourage students to read the conversation before writing.

> **Answers**
> 2 matter   3 hurts   4 hot   5 temperature   6 down

3 Read the Exam tip as a class. Encourage the students to read the sentences and think of some possible answers before they look at the expressions (a–c). Point out that they need to choose two correct expressions.

> **Answers**
> 1 a & b   2 a & c   3 a & b   4 b & c   5 a & c

Exam task

Remind students to read the first part of the conversation and think of a possible answer before they read A, B and C.

> **Answers**
> 1 A   2 B   3 C   4 A   5 B

Writing

Part 6

Grammar – Present perfect with *for* & *since*

1 Elicit what is the matter with Lena. Point out the present perfect can also describe an action or situation which started in the past and continues into the present. Refer students to the Grammar reference on page 88.

> **Answers**
> 1 three days ago   2 yes   3 She's afraid of her dentist.

2 Looking at the conversation in Exercise 1 students say when we use *for* and *since*: *for* + a period of time and *since* + a point in time. Students keep a list in their notebooks, e.g.

for	since
3 days	9 o'clock
a week, etc.	Tuesday, etc.

Students can add the words in the exercise to their list.

> **Answers**
> 1 since   2 since   3 since   4 for   5 for   6 since

Further practice

Students rewrite the sentences so that they are true for them, e.g. *I've had short hair for three years.* Then, in pairs, they ask and answer questions about their sentences using *How long ...?*, e.g. *How long have you had short hair? I've had short hair for three years.*

3 Read the Exam tip as a class. Remind students that their spelling has to be correct in this part. If they have trouble spelling certain words, they should keep a list in their notebook and test themselves on the spellings regularly.

> **Answers**
> 2 rubber   3 birthday   4 friends   5 house   6 mobile

Exam task

Ask the students to look at the Exam task instructions first and to say what the sentences are about (health). Remind the students that Writing Part 6 is a like a crossword puzzle. Their word needs to fit the number of spaces exactly.

> **Answers**
> 1 hospital   2 nurse   3 ambulance   4 medicine   5 exercise

Personal feelings

Listening

Part 3

Vocabulary – Adjectives

1 Encourage the students to look at the faces first and to say the feeling before they read the words.

> **Answers**
> 2 hungry   3 bored   4 angry   5 sick   6 unhappy

2 Point out there may be different possible answers. Encourage students to compare their answers and feelings.

> **Suggested answers**
> 2 I feel very hungry and a little angry.
> 3 I feel great and very lucky.
> 4 I feel sorry.
> 5 I feel afraid.

Further practice

Students choose two new words from Exercise 1 and write about a situation when they feel like this. In small groups, the students take turns to read their situation and to say how they feel in each one, e.g. *You've just eaten too many cakes. How do you feel? I feel really sick.*

3 🔊 37 Ask students to say what they have to do in this part (listen to two friends talking and choose the correct answer A–C). Read the Exam tip as a class. Point out that the students will hear the other two answers but they should think about why these answers are incorrect.

> **Answer**
> 3 A: you do one activity in the afternoon
> B: you can choose two activities in the morning

> **Recording script**
>
> Lynda: I've just done the most amazing Healthy Living Day at the sports centre.
> Craig: Cool! But what's a Healthy Living Day?
> Lynda: Well, you learn to live in a healthy way. <u>Everyone does three activities. In the morning, you can choose two different indoor activities</u> and <u>in the afternoon, you can try one activity outdoors</u>. I had great fun mountain biking in the afternoon.

Exam task

🔊 38 Encourage the students to read the questions and the answers first before they listen. Play the recording twice. Encourage the students to compare their answers and to say why the other two options are incorrect.

> **Answers**
> 1 C 2 C 3 A 4 B 5 B

> **Recording script**
>
> *Listen to Lynda talking to her friend Craig about a Healthy Living Day at a sports centre.*
>
> *For each question, choose the right answer (A, B, or C)*
>
> Lynda: I've just done the most amazing Healthy Living Day at the sports centre.
> Craig: Cool! But what's a Healthy Living Day?
> Lynda: Well, you learn to live in a healthy way. (0) <u>Everyone does three activities</u>. In the morning, you can choose two different indoor activities and in the afternoon, you can try one activity outdoors. I had great fun mountain biking in the afternoon.
> Craig: Sounds like hard work! Why did you do it?

> Lynda: (1) <u>I wanted to do a new activity</u>, so I went with my cousin Georgia. She doesn't do enough exercise and she wanted to try a different sport. We made lots of new friends.
> Craig: Were you both really tired when you finished?
> Lynda: Georgia was and she didn't feel very well. I was OK but (2) <u>I needed something to drink</u>.
> Craig: How much was it? Was it expensive?
> Lynda: No, it was £20 for adults, £15 for under 16s but we're members, (3) <u>so it was only £10 for us</u>.
> Craig: That's not bad. So, when's the next day? I'd love to go. I know I'm free most Saturdays after 14th April.
> Lynda: Oh, I've just booked a place for July 5th but (4) <u>I think the next one is on 28th May</u>.
> Craig: Brilliant! I'll come to the same one as you! Are you going to go cycling again?
> Lynda: Not this time. (5) <u>I'm going to do advanced skateboarding</u>. I wanted to try windsurfing but that group is full.
> Craig: Wow! I'd like to do that too!

Speaking

Part 1

1 Students describe what they can see in the photos. Have a brief discussion on what the students do to keep fit and healthy, e.g. *What do you do to keep fit? Are you a member of a sports club or gym? What do you do to keep healthy? Do you eat well?* Students think of some of the trainer's questions but they should not write their questions yet.

> **Suggested answers**
> b What's your surname?   c Where do you live?   d How long have you lived there?   e When were you born?   f What school do you go to?   g What are your favourite sports?   h What's your favourite food?   i Have you got any health problems? j What do you do in your free time?

2 🔊 39 Point out that the students will hear the information in order and they will need to spell Billy's surname and the name of his school correctly as the spelling is given. They write the answers on the form.

> **Answers**
> 2 Bladden   3 54 Hendon Street   4 4 years   5 24 May 1999
> 6 Petersdale High School   7 hockey and basketball   8 salad, fish and vegetables   9 No   10 meet friends, ride my bike, go to the skate park, go to the cinema

> **Recording script**
>
> Trainer: Good morning! I'm Ellie. Before we start, I'd like to ask you some questions, please.
> Billy: OK.
> Trainer: Now, what's your name?
> Billy: It's William but my friends call me (1) <u>Billy</u>.
> Trainer: I'll put Billy then. And what's your surname, Billy?
> Billy: It's Bladden.
> Trainer: How do you spell that?
> Billy: (2) <u>It's B–L–A–double D–E–N</u>
> Trainer: Where do you live?

Billy:	I live here in Petersdale at (3) <u>54 Hendon Street</u>. That's H–E–N–D–O–N
Trainer:	And how long have you lived there?
Billy:	(4) <u>For about four years</u>, I think.
Trainer:	When were you born?
Billy:	(5) <u>24th May 1999</u>. Am I too young for the club?
Trainer:	No, that's fine. We've got a special programme for kids of your age. What school do you go to?
Billy:	(6) <u>I go to Petersdale High School</u>. That's P–E–T–E–R–S–D–A–L–E.
Trainer:	What sports do you like?
Billy:	(7) <u>I like team sports like hockey and basketball</u>.
Trainer:	Now, Billy, what's your favourite food?
Billy:	(8) <u>I like salad, fish and vegetables best</u>.
Trainer:	That sounds healthy! OK, have you got any health problems?
Billy:	(9) <u>No</u>, I don't think so.
Trainer:	Now the last question ... tell me something about your weekend.
Billy:	Well, (10) <u>I often get up early on Saturday and meet my friends. We sometimes ride our bikes or go to the skate park. On Saturday afternoon, I sometimes go to the cinema with my family. I love cartoons. On Sunday, I usually stay at home and I do my homework.</u>
Trainer:	Thanks Billy. I think we have the perfect sports programme for you. On Tuesdays, you'll ...

Katerina:	Ah! It's P–E–T–R–O–V–A
Examiner:	Where do you come from?
Katerina:	I'm sorry. I don't understand.
Examiner:	Where do you live?
Katerina:	Sorry. I live in the Czech Republic.
Examiner:	Do you study English at school?
Katerina:	Yes, I do.
Examiner:	What subjects do you like best?
Katerina:	I like sport.
Examiner:	Why?
Katerina:	Because I love running and I'm good at it.
Examiner:	What's your favourite meal of the day?
Katerina:	Can you say that again, please?
Examiner:	What's your favourite meal of the day?
Katerina:	My favourite meal? I like dinner best, I think.
Examiner:	What do you normally have for dinner?
Katerina:	We often have soup or salad.
Examiner:	Who usually cooks in your house?
Katerina:	My mum or my dad, or sometimes I cook.
Examiner:	<u>Tell me something about your weekend</u>.
Katerina:	Well, I often go running on Saturday morning with my dad. In the afternoon, I meet my friends and we go to the town centre. On Sunday, we sometimes have lunch at my grandmother's house.
Examiner:	Thank you, Katerina. In the next part ...

3 With a weaker class, it might be necessary to play the recording several times.

> **Answers**
>
> b) What's your surname, Billy?   c) How do you spell that?
> d) Where do you live?   e) How long have you lived there?
> f) When were you born?   g) What school do you go to?
> h) What sports do you like?   i) What's your favourite food?
> j) Have you got any health problems?   k) Tell me something about your weekend.

4 🔊 40 In Speaking Part 1, the examiner will ask personal information questions similar to the types of questions you might ask someone when you meet them for the first time. The examiner will always ask each candidate to spell their surname so students should practise this.

> **Answers**
>
> a, b, c, d, k

> **Recording script**
>
> | | |
> |---|---|
> | Examiner: | Good morning! |
> | Katerina: | Good morning! |
> | Examiner: | <u>What's your name?</u> |
> | Katerina: | It's Katerina. |
> | Examiner: | <u>And what's your surname?</u> |
> | Katerina: | It's Petrova. |
> | Examiner: | <u>How do you spell that?</u> |
> | Katerina: | Sorry? |
> | Examiner: | How do you spell that? |

5 Read the Exam tip as a class. Make sure the students can pronounce the expressions well.

> **Answers**
>
> Sorry?
> I'm sorry. I don't understand.
> Can you say that again, please?

Exam task

Remind the students to use the expressions *I'm sorry, Pardon?* etc. if they don't understand. For more Speaking Part 1 practice see the Speaking Section on page 91.

> **Suggested answer**
>
> | | |
> |---|---|
> | Student A: | Good morning! |
> | Student B: | Good morning! |
> | Student A: | What's your name? |
> | Student B: | It's Ruben. |
> | Student A: | And what's your surname? |
> | Student B: | It's Fernandez. |
> | Student A: | How do you spell that? |
> | Student B: | I'm sorry. I don't understand. |
> | Student A: | How do you spell that? |
> | Student B: | Ah! It's F-E-R-N-A-N-D-E-Z. |
> | Student A: | Where do you live? |
> | Student B: | I live in Spain. |
> | Student A: | Tell me something about your weekend. |
> | Student B: | I often play basketball on Saturday morning with my team. In the afternoon, I meet my friends and we ride our bikes or we go swimming. On Sunday, we usually have lunch with my aunt and cousins. |
> | Student A: | Thank you. |

Unit objectives

KEY FOR SCHOOLS TOPICS	communication, appliances
GRAMMAR	the passive: present and past, passive or active
VOCABULARY	communication and technology, describing objects
READING	Part 4: Choosing the correct person
WRITING	Part 7: Using the correct form of the verb
LISTENING	Part 2: Listening to the words around the answers
SPEAKING	Part 2: Asking your partner for clarification

Communication

Listening

Part 2

Vocabulary – Communication & technology

1 Encourage the students to look at the photo first and to say what they can see.

> **Answers**
>
> A PC Bang is a kind of internet café or games centre where you can meet your friends and play computer games.

2 With a weaker class, write the verbs on the board in the wrong order first to help the students.

> **Answers**
>
> 2 play   3 download   4 chat   5 text   6 call   7 use

3 In pairs, students ask and answer the questions for themselves. Monitor, making sure they are answering in full sentences and giving more information where possible.

4 🔊 41 Check students understand the words in the exercise before they listen. Students need to tick the presents the friends got (and not necessarily all the words they hear). Play the recording. Students check their answers with a partner. Check as a class after the second listening.

> **Answers**
>
> Malcolm: MP3 player   Pete: DVD
> Katie: printer   Reeta: Games console

> **Recording script**
>
> Brother: I've just seen Malcolm. He's got a new mobile phone.
> Mara: No, he hasn't. It's his brother's but (1) his MP3 player is new. Have you seen it?
> Brother: No, I haven't. It was his sister's birthday yesterday. What did she get?
> Mara: Who Katie? (2) She usually asks for DVDs but this year she got a printer.
>
> Brother: Cool! And what about your friend Pete? Has he spent his birthday money yet?
> Mara: Yes, he has. (3) He wanted to buy a games console but he bought a DVD instead.
> Brother: Really? We've got an old games console he can have.
> Mara: That's true. (4) My friend Reeta has just bought a new games console. It's amazing! You can even watch DVDs on it.

Exam task

🔊 42 Students say what they have to do in this part (listen to Helen and match the people 1–5 with the thing they use most often (A–H)). Read the Exam tip as a class.

Remind students that Helen will talk about each member of the family in order. She may mention two of the favourite things for each person but only one will be correct. Play the recording twice.

> **Answers**
>
> 1 E   2 F   3 A   4 G   5 D

> **Recording script**
>
> *Listen to Helen talking to a friend about her family.*
>
> *What is each person's favourite thing?*
>
> *For questions 1–5, write a letter A–H next to each person.*
>
> Boy: Hi, Helen. What's the matter?
> Helen: I've just broken my dad's CD player and it's his favourite thing.
> Boy: Oh, no! Your family love new technology, don't they?
> Helen: Yes. It started when (1) my mum bought a digital camera. She likes it more than anything else. Then we had to buy a laptop to look at the photos.
> Boy: And I suppose your sister's favourite thing is the laptop.
> Helen: Well, she likes playing games on it but (2) I think she prefers our TV. She spends hours watching cartoons on it.
> Boy: Is your brother's MP3 player still his favourite thing?
> Helen: No, now (3) it's his mobile. He's had it since his birthday.
> Boy: What did he do with the MP3 player?
> Helen: He gave it to our grandma so she could listen to the news. (4) Then she was given a digital radio. She says that's her favourite thing. She can listen to programmes from all over the world.
> Boy: Does your grandfather still get DVDs from the library?
> Helen: He doesn't need to. We taught him how to download films and now (5) he says our laptop is the best thing in the world!

Grammar – The passive: present

6 Ask students if the cartoons are true for them. After the students have answered the questions, elicit how we form the passive (object + *be* + past participle + *by* subject) and when we use it, i.e. when we do not know who or what does the action or when we are not interested in who or what does or did the action. Refer the students to the Grammar reference on page 89 if necessary.

> **Answers**
>
> 1 Yes, his friends. 2 No, we don't and it isn't important.
> 3 Sentence 2. 4 We form the passive with *be* + the past participle.

7 Encourage the students to complete the sentences first. Remind them to use the correct form of *be* in each sentence, e.g. 2 *Films are* but 3 *This is.* Then check students understand the meaning of the words.

> **Answers**
>
> 2 are watched; screen 3 is needed; keyboard
> 4 is downloaded; Internet 5 is moved, is clicked; mouse
> 6 are sent; email address.

8 Invite a brief class discussion on Twitter before the students do this exercise: *What is it? Who reads the messages? Do any of the students use it?* Students read the complete text first before writing.

> **Answers**
>
> 1 is used 2 aren't (are not) spoken 3 are sent 4 aren't (are not) called 5 are known 6 isn't (is not) used 7 are followed

Further practice

Write these skeleton questions on the board:

1 you / send / more than 20 texts a day?
2 all your homework / do / on a computer?
3 your computer / turn on for most of the day?
4 you / give / computer games, programmes, books, etc. for your birthday?
5 your favourite webpage / make / by you?
6 most of your clothes and books / buy / online?

In pairs, students write complete questions using the passive. Then, they take turns to ask and answer the questions.

> See the Workbook and CD ROM for further practice on Grammar & Vocabulary.

Reading

Part 4

1 Invite a brief class discussion on what ICT is and whether the students study it at school.

> **Suggested**
>
> Yes, we study ICT at school. We do it on Monday and Wednesday.

2 Ask the students to look at the Exam task and to say what they have to do in this part: read three short paragraphs about three different people and answer seven questions. The answers to the questions are the names of the three different people. Ask the students what the Exam task is about, (three young people from different parts of the world talking about technology). Read the Exam tip as a class.

> **Suggested**
>
> 1 *A Isra* is the correct answer; she says *We also do ICT on Wednesday mornings after science.*
> 2 *C Ida* is not the correct answer because she says *We don't study ICT as a school subject.*

Exam task

Encourage students to read the complete article before they answer the questions. They should underline the important words in the questions and the answers in the article. Remind them not to choose an answer because the same words are in the text. Students compare their answers by saying, e.g. *I think ... is correct because in the article it says ... .*

> **Answers**
>
> 1 A (nobody buys text books)
> 2 C (Last Wednesday ... in science ... we looked for information online)
> 3 B (finish my homework quickly and then play football with my friends.)
> 4 C (there won't be any books)
> 5 B (Our history teacher ... often downloads interesting videos)
> 6 B (we sometimes go to the computer room)
> 7 A (We also do ICT on Wednesday mornings after science)

★ **CLIL** ICT / Maths: In small groups, students design a technology questionnaire to find out what their classmates think about new technology, if they use it and what they think technology will be like in the future. Give the students some example questions but encourage the groups to write some of their own, e.g. *1 Do you use new technology at school? 2 Do you often use the Internet to find information? Are you interested in new technology? 3 Does your family use new technology? 4 What will technology be like in the future? 5 Will we use books in the future?* Students use a web tool like Survey Monkey to create their questionnaire and then encourage their classmates to complete it. Each group should then present their results to the class using spreadsheet software like Microsoft Excel to produce graphs, charts and diagrams to illustrate the results, etc.

Grammar

Grammar – The passive: past

1 Encourage the students to look at the pictures and to say what the objects are before they read the sentences. When the students have finished the exercise, ask them to underline the verb forms and elicit that these are all examples of the past passive. If necessary, refer the students to the Grammar reference on page 89.

> **Answers**
>
> 1 B Walkman 2 C laptop computer 3 A telephone

2 With books closed, ask students *How do you get news and messages?* Elicit different ways, e.g. mobile phone, TV, email, etc. Ask them to try and say what order these things were invented. With books open, the students check their ideas and write complete sentences like the example. Remind the students to use the past passive.

Answers

2 The first person was phoned in 1876.
3 TVs were watched for the first time in 1925.
4 Computers were sold in shops in 1951.
5 The Internet was used for the first time in 1969.

Further practice

In small groups, students research the history of a piece of technology or service, e.g. the iPod or MP3 player, the mobile phone, the Internet, messaging, etc. They then use a web tool like Timetoast to create an online history timeline. If possible, they should include some sentences in the passive.

3 Point out that these sentences are in both the present and past passive. There may be mistakes with the form (*is* instead of *are*) or the use (present instead of past).

Answers

2 is ~~call~~ = called   3 ~~is~~ given = was   4 was ~~writed~~ = written
5 it's ~~make~~ = made   6 ~~are~~ made = were

4 Remind students when we use the passive by writing two example sentences on the board and asking questions, e.g.
1 I love watching films. (Who loves watching films? I do) ACTIVE
2 I'm often given DVDs for my birthday. (Who gives her the DVDs? We don't know.) PASSIVE
Encourage the students to read the complete conversation before they choose the correct answers.

Answers

1 I was woken   2 did she do   3 was given   4 decided
5 was sent   6 Do you want   7 love   8 isn't called

Speaking

Part 2

1 🔊 43 Encourage the students to read the advert for the computer course first and predict what information is missing in each space before they listen.

Answers

2 make web pages   3 4   4 45   5 6th   6 454699

Recording script

Max: Hi, Inge! How are you?
Inge: Hi, Max! Not bad and you?
Max: OK. Look, you've just done a computer course, haven't you?
Inge: Yes, I did one two weeks ago. It was brilliant.

Max: I'd like to do a course with my brother. Is it for children?
Inge: Yes, (1) it's for eleven to sixteen year olds.
Max: Great! And what do you do on the course?
Inge: Well, (2) you're taught how to make web pages.
Max: Sounds good! How many students are there per teacher?
Inge: That's the best thing. (3) There are only four so you get a lot of help. And of course the teachers are really good.
Max: Cool! How much is it? Is it expensive?
Inge: Not really. It's £15 for each class so (4) if you do all three, it's £45.
Max: And when does it start?
Inge: Do you mean the date or the time?
Max: The date.
Inge: Oh, I think the next course starts (5) on 6th June but you'll have to check that.
Max: How can I get more information?
Inge: (6) The phone number is 454699.
Max: Thanks, Inge.

---

2 Encourage the students to write the questions before they listen again. They will check their answers in Exercise 3.

Suggested

2 What do/can you do/learn on the course?
3 Are the classes big? / Are there big classes? / How many students are there per teacher?
4 Is it expensive?
5 When does the first class / next course / it start?
6 How can I get more information?

3 Play the recording twice if necessary. Point out that Max is asking a friend for more information about a course. In the Speaking Part 2 exam, the students will also have to ask for more information about an activity or event.

Answers

2 What do you do on the course?
3 How many students are there per teacher?
4 How much is it? Is it expensive?
5 When does it start?
6 How can I get more information?

4 With a stronger class, see if the students can remember Inge's question without reading the conversation.

Answer

Do you mean the date or the time?

5 Read the Exam tip as a class and point out that the students can ask for clarification in the exam, e.g. *I don't understand.*, *Can you repeat that, please?* or *Do you mean ...?* With a stronger class, encourage the students to try to complete the questions without looking at the words. Students then take turns to ask and answer questions about the computer course. Remind the students to ask for clarification using the questions in this exercise.

Answers

2 place   3 price   4 website address   5 prize

Exam task

Read the complete exam rubric to the class:

Student A, here is some information about a web page competition for schools.

Student B, you don't know anything about the web page competition for schools, so ask student A some questions about it. Use these words to help you.

Now, student B, ask your questions about the web page competition, and student A, you answer them.

Web page competition for schools	Web page competition for schools
 Make a web page about your school and win new computers for your school! Open to all students under 16 Competition ends 17th June jon@webcompetition.com	 ◆ what / do ? ◆ for children ? ◆ when / finish ? ◆ email address ? ◆ prize ?

Student B, here is some information about a new computer game.

Student A, you don't know anything about the new computer game, so ask student B some questions about it. Use these words to help you.

Now, student A, ask your questions about the new computer game, and student B, you answer them.

Rock band!	New computer game
An exciting new computer game Make your own group and play cool music  For 2 – 4 players Only £20! On sale online only www.rockband.com	 ◆ name ? ◆ what / do ? ◆ where / buy ? ◆ price ? ◆ website ?

Refer the students to the speaking section if they need more practice with this part.

> **Suggested**
>
> B: What do I have to do?
> A: Make a web page about your school.
> B: Is it for children?
> A: Yes, it's open to all students under 16.
> B: When does the competition finish?
> A: The competition ends 17 June.
> B: Is there an email address?
> A: Yes, it's jon@webcompetition.com
> B: What's the prize?
> A: You can win new computers for your school!
>
> A: What's the name of the game?
> B: It's Rock Band.

> A: What do I have to do?
> B: Make your own group and play cool music.
> A: Where can I buy it?
> B: It's on sale online.
> A: How much is it?
> B: It's only £20!
> A: Is there a website?
> B: Yes, it's www.rockband.com

Appliances

Writing

Part 7

Vocabulary – Describing objects

1 Students look at the pictures first and say what they can see before they read the sentences. Remind the students to count the number of spaces to see how many letters are missing. Check they spell these words correctly.

> **Answers**
>
> 2 case 3 lamp 4 hairdryer 5 fridge 6 cooker

2 Encourage the students to underline the examples of *made of, by* and *in* in the descriptions in Exercise 1 and to say when we use each one before they match 1–3 with a–c.

> **Answers**
>
> 1c 2a 3b

3 Ask the students what they have to do in this Reading Part 1 Exam task: read two emails and write one word in each space. Point out that in some Exam tasks (e.g. Unit 6), there's one email but in others, like this one, there are two emails. Read the Exam tip as a class. Remind the students that they should look at the subject of the sentence (*I, you, he,* etc), the tense (present, past, future) and, if it is a verb with two parts, the part given (e.g. *Today I .... wearing* or *Did you .... to the park yesterday?*). With a weaker class, point out where the mistakes are.

> **Answer**
>
> 2 my cousin ~~are~~ = was 3 We ~~was~~ talking = were 4 I ~~likes~~ it = like 5 It ~~have~~ bluetooth = has 6 It ~~don't~~ weigh = doesn't 7 it ~~were~~ made = was 8 programme ~~start~~ = starts

Exam task

Encourage the students to read both emails first and say what the problem in the first email is (Bruno's lost his sister's MP3 player) and the solution in the second (Lizzie will get the MP3 player from Jason). Remind the students that they should only write ONE word in each space and that their spelling of these words MUST be correct.

> **Answers**
>
> 1 was 2 a 3 at 4 you 5 in 6 has 7 took / drove / brought 8 to 9 when 10 or

> See the Workbook and CD ROM for further practice on Grammar & Vocabulary.

Revision: Units 1 & 2

Unit 1

1 Put these words in order to make questions. Then write your own answers.

wake up / What time / do / you and your family / ?
What time do you and your family wake up? We wake up at 7 o'clock.

1 your best friend / How / to school / go / does / ?
....

2 and / brothers / sisters / have / How many / got / you / ?
....

3 school / What time / does / finish / ?
....

4 your homework / do / you / When / do / ?
....

5 do / you and your friends / Where / after school / go / ?
....

6 cousin / is / your favourite / Who / ?
....

7 you / How / do / the town centre / go / to / ?
....

8 have / Where / do / on a school day / lunch / you / ?
....

2 Complete these sentences with a suitable verb.

I usually w *ake up* .... before my alarm clock rings.

1 I w.................. to school with my friends. We don't go by bus.
2 We s.................. school at eight a.m.
3 I don't go home for lunch. I h.................. lunch at school.
4 I usually g.................. home from school at five o'clock.
5 I always d.................. my homework before dinner.
6 After dinner, I w.................. TV with my family.
7 During the week, I g.................. to bed at ten o'clock.

Unit 2

1 Rewrite these sentences with the word in brackets.

I play tennis with my uncle. (every Saturday)
I play tennis with my uncle every Saturday

1 My mum takes photographs of us. (often)
....

2 We sleep in a tent. (never)
....

3 I'm late for my drawing classes. (sometimes)
....

4 I go to the cinema with my friends. (twice a month)
....

5 My friends do after-school activities. (every day)
....

6 My best friend draws pictures. (often)
....

2 Complete these sentences with the words in the box.

| playing | writing | watching | drawing |
| going | listening | sleeping | collecting | taking |

I prefer ....*playing*.... sports to watching them.

1 My brother's interested in .... stamps. He's now got about 500.
2 My best friend is really good at .... pictures.
3 My family and I enjoy .... photos when we go on holiday.
4 I hate .... in a tent, I prefer hotels.
5 I love .... films on Sunday afternoon.
6 I like .... to music when I travel by train.
7 I'm not interested in .... to concerts. They're too expensive.
8 I hate .... emails. I prefer phoning my friends.

Revision: Units 3 & 4

Unit 3

1 Complete the email with ONE word in each space.

From: Wendi

To: Nicole

There (1) .... only one place to have breakfast on Sunday and that's my grandma's house. She's got (2) .... beautiful house with (3) .... amazing garden. There (4) .... some chairs and a table outside and we often eat there. She often makes omelettes but if there aren't (5) .... eggs, we have (6) .... homemade bread and jam. What's your favourite place to have breakfast?

2 Use the words to write sentences which are true for you.

help at home   *I have to help at home. I have to tidy tidy my room.*

1 do a lot of homework   ....

2 wear a school uniform   ....

3 make your breakfast   ....

4 work hard at school   ....

5 get up early for school   ....

6 go to bed early   ....

3 Read the sentence and write the word.

I use this every morning to wash myself.   s .h. .o. .w. .e. .r.

1 We put all the plates, cups and glasses.   c ....
in this

2 I look at this when I brush my hair.   m ....

3 If it's too dark, turn this on.   l ....

4 All my family sit on this and watch   s ....
TV together.

5 I sit at this and do my homework.   d ....

6 At night, you lie down on this and   b ....
go to sleep.

7 You have to put milk, cheese and   f ....
meat in this to keep cold.

8 To make a cake, fry an egg or boil   c ....
vegetables, you need this.

Unit 4

1 Circle the correct words in *italics*.

My brother *clean /('s cleaning)*his bike right now.

1 I'm sorry. I *don't understand / 'm not understanding*.

2 We *don't go / aren't going* skiing every weekend.

3 My family *watches / is watching* a film twice a week.

4 Let's go out. It *doesn't rain / isn't raining* now.

5 Our school team *wins / 's winning* the match at the moment.

6 My sister *never wears / is never wearing* trainers for school.

7 John can't come to football practice. He *studies / 's studying* for a test.

8 What *does that boy wear / is that boy wearing*? He looks strange.

2 Complete these sentences with the words in the box.

| ~~coat~~ sweater trainers helmet |
| socks jeans costume |

It's cold today. You need to wear a ....*coat*............ outside.

1 You can't wear those boots to go running. Put on your .... !

2 I want to go swimming. Where is my swimming ....

3 When you ride your bike, please put on your ....

4 You aren't wearing .... so your shoes are uncomfortable .

5 We have to wear grey trousers for school, we can't wear ....

6 It's very hot. Why don't you take off your ....

Revision: Units 5 & 6

Unit 5

1 Complete these sentences with the past simple form of the verb and *at, on* or *in*.

My cousin _____*arrived*_____ (arrive) home _____*at*_____ 8.30 p.m.

1 I _____ (be) born _____ 3rd May 2001.

2 We _____ (not play) football _____ the weekend.

3 What _____ you _____ (do) _____ night on holiday?

4 My friends _____ (not be) at school _____ 9 o'clock.

5 The new cinema _____ (open) in our town _____ Saturday.

6 _____ you _____ (have) a good time _____ the morning?

7 My teacher _____ (not work) in my school _____ 2013.

8 My brother _____ (begin) learning Chinese _____ October.

2 Read the sentences and write the places.

I often watch films here with my family.
c _i_ _n_ _e_ _m_ _a_.

1 I often go here to borrow books. l ___ ___ ___ ___ ___

2 We saw a great play here last week.
t ___ ___ ___ ___ ___ ___

3 My friends go here twice a week for basketball practice. s ___ ___ ___ ___ ___   c ___ ___ ___ ___ ___

4 We saw an exhibition about Japan at this place.
m ___ ___ ___ ___ ___

5 When we want to buy different things, we go here. d ___ ___ ___ ___ ___ ___ ___   s ___ ___ ___ ___

6 My dad always buys his newspapers here.
n ___ ___ ___ ___ ___

7 When I leave school, I want to study here.
u ___ ___ ___ ___ ___ ___ ___

8 My mum doesn't buy books online she buys them here. b ___ ___ ___ ___ ___

Unit 6

1 Complete the sentences so they are true for you. Use comparative or superlative adjectives.

I / student in my class (fast)
I'm not the fastest student in my class. My best friend is faster than me.

1 My dad's car / my uncle's car (slow)
_____

2 My school / in my town (big)
_____

3 The countryside / the town (beautiful)
_____

4 Trains / planes (comfortable)
_____

5 Science / maths (easy)
_____

6 The car / transport in the world (bad)
_____

7 The school library / the library in my town (quiet)
_____

8 My city / in my country (large)
_____

2 Circle the correct words in *italics*.

When the (*traffic lights*) / *roundabout* are red, you must stop.

1 I often *ride* / *walk* my bike to school.

2 Yesterday we went to the cinema *by* / *on* foot.

3 We drove my aunt to Madrid airport and she took the *plane* / *tram* to New York.

4 I would love to *sail* / *fly* around the world in a small boat.

5 If you want to cross the road, use the *car park* / *crossing*.

6 My sister learnt to *drive* / *ride* a car last year.

7 We were late so we went to the theatre *by* / *on* taxi.

8 In my town, there are three *squares* / *bridges* over the river.

Revision: Units 7 & 8

Unit 7

1 Circle the correct words in *italics*.

It's very hot in here. You *should* / *shouldn't* take off your sweater.

1 It's too dark in here. We *can't* / *mustn't* see anything.

2 You can't write your answers in pen. You *must* / *mustn't* write in pencil.

3 Shh! You *couldn't* / *mustn't* talk loudly in the library.

4 You *shouldn't* / *can't* worry so much about the exam.

5 My cousin is good at languages. She *can* / *could* speak English, French, Spanish and German.

6 My little brother is afraid of water so he *can't* / *mustn't* swim at all.

7 I left my books at school so I *couldn't* / *mustn't* do my homework last night.

8 When my dad was young, he *could* / *should* play football brilliantly.

2 Match the description with the school subject.

1 You learn how to draw pictures.

2 You learn about things that happened in the past.

3 You study countries and their capital cities in this subject.

4 Some students play instruments in this class.

5 You learn how to speak a language in this lesson.

6 You study animals and plants or electricity and machines.

7 You need to work with numbers in this subject.

a music
b art
c English
d maths
e science
f geography
g history

Unit 8

1 Write complete questions in the correct form of the past continuous. Then write your own answer.

you / climb a tree at 6 p.m. on Saturday?
Were you climbing a tree at 6 p.m. on Saturday? No, I wasn't. I was riding my bike.

1 your classmates / speak English at 11 a.m. yesterday?

2 you / have a rest at 3 p.m. on Sunday?

3 your friends and you / talk when the class started?

4 you / sleep last night at 11 p.m.?

5 your dad / make breakfast when you woke up this morning?

6 it / rain when you left home this morning?

7 you / have lunch at 2 p.m. yesterday?

2 Complete the sentences with the words in the box.

French   capital cities   a rest
the Amazon rainforest   many different languages
new dishes   on a campsite

I lived in France when I was 7 years old so I learnt ...... French ....

1 You look tired. You should have ....
2 I love food from all over the world. I love trying ....
3 We often stay .... and sleep in our tent.
4 I'm interested in plants and animals. I'd love to explore ....
5 My uncle has lived in many different countries so he can speak ....
6 My parents went to London, Rome and Paris last year. They like visiting ....

Revision: Units 9 & 10

Unit 9

1 Complete these conversations. Use *be going to* and the verb in brackets.

A: Why don't we go to the cinema after school?

B: I'm sorry I can't. I *'m going to do* (do) my homework.

1 A: We .... (ride) our bikes. Would you like to come?

  B: .... you .... (ask) Pippa to come, too?

2 A: I .... (play) football on Friday afternoon. What about you?

  B: I .... (not do) anything. I .... (have) a rest.

3 A: My brother .... (play) in a concert. Why don't you come and watch?

  B: Cool! .... he .... (play) the piano?

4 A: We .... (watch) a DVD at Jake's house on Saturday afternoon. Are you free?

  B: No, sorry, I .... (study) for my history test.

5 A: Should I take an umbrella?

  B: No! It .... (not rain) today.

2 Complete the sentences with the correct form of the words in bold.

I'm interested in **music**. I'd like to be a *musician* .... when I'm older.

1 My brother plays the **guitar** in a band. He's a brilliant ....

2 My cousin **acts** in plays in New York. He's a famous ....

3 I don't like **dancing** because I'm a terrible ....

4 You're very good at **art**. You should be an ....

5 Our teacher enjoys taking **photos**. He's a good ....

6 My best friend can't play the **drums** well. He isn't a good ....

Unit 10

1 Circle the correct words in italics.

It's very windy. Be careful – you (may) / won't lose your hat!

1 Don't worry. We won't / may be late. It's only five o'clock.

2 I'm not sure but we may / will go to Portugal in the spring.

3 Put on warm clothes. It will / won't be cold outside. It's winter.

4 There are some clouds in the sky. It won't / may rain later.

5 Let's play tennis now. It won't / will be dark later.

6 I'm certain you will / may win the race. You're the fastest runner.

2 Write complete first conditional sentences.

If it be sunny / I go to the lake.
If it's sunny, I'll go to the lake.

1 If the water be cold / I not go swimming.
....

2 I read a book / if I not go swimming.
....

3 If I finish the book / I talk to my sister.
....

4 I listen to music / if my sister not want to talk.
....

5 If I not have my MP3 player / I go for a walk.
....

3 Complete this text with the words in the box.

farm	wood	hill	field	gate	river	path

My uncle is a farmer. We often stay on his **(0)** *farm* .... in the summer. In front of his house, there's a big **(1)** .... with cows and horses in it. My uncle gets angry if we don't close the **(2)** .... There's also a **(3)** .... with all kinds of trees. We often go for a walk there. My mum says we have to walk on the **(4)** .... so we don't get lost. When it's hot and sunny, we go swimming in the **(5)** .... I also love walking up the **(6)** .... and then running down it again.

Revision: Units 11 & 12

Unit 11

1 Complete these sentences with the present perfect form of the verb in brackets.

My brother _has broken_ (break) his arm.

1 We .... already .... (visit) the Science museum.
2 I .... (not brush) my teeth yet.
3 .... you .... (see) that film yet?
4 I .... (know) my best friend since I was five.
5 My teacher .... (not arrive) yet.

2 Circle the correct words in *italics*.

Hi Lianne,

So sorry that I haven't answered your message *already* / (*yet*) but I've been really busy studying for my exams. Have you finished your exams **(1)** *just* / *yet*? I'm so excited that you're coming to stay with me. Have you bought your train ticket **(2)** *just* / *yet*? My mum has **(3)** *just* / *yet* booked tickets for the Healthy Body exhibition but we haven't decided where to eat afterwards **(4)** *already* / *yet*.

Anyway, I have to go because it's **(5)** *already* / *yet* 6 o'clock and I haven't done my homework **(6)** *just* / *yet*.

Best wishes,

Alicia

3 Match the sentences (1–8) with the replies (a–h).

1 I'm thirsty.
2 I'm tired.
3 We're bored.
4 I'm really hungry.
5 I'm sorry I'm late.
6 I feel sick.
7 I'm afraid of the dark.
8 We're happy to see you.

a) How about playing a game?
b) Don't worry. I'll turn on the lamp.
c) You shouldn't eat so many cakes.
d) Why don't you have something to drink?
e) I'm pleased, too.
f) You should go to bed earlier.
g) It doesn't matter but don't do it again.
h) Make a sandwich!

Unit 12

1 Write complete sentences in the present passive.

My brother / call / Kieran.
My brother is called Kieran.

1 My shoes / made of leather. ....
2 I / give money for my birthday. ....
3 Rugby / not play at my school. ....
4 English / speak all over the world ....
5 CDs / not sell here anymore. ....

2 Write complete sentences in the past passive.

Our house / build 200 years ago.
Our house was built 200 years ago.

1 This book / write by my uncle.
....
2 My mum / teach how to cook at school.
....
3 We / tell an interesting story this morning.
....
4 I / drive to school yesterday.
....
5 My friends / not invite to the party.
....

3 Complete the sentences with the words in the box.

~~write~~   send   use   download   call   play   chat

My parents _write_ .... emails to their friends every night.

1 I don't phone my friends very often. I usually .... them a message.
2 We usually have to .... the Internet to do our homework.
3 After dinner, I turn on my computer and I .... with my friends over the Internet.
4 I don't .... computer games but my brother loves them.
5 When we're bored, we sometimes .... a film from the Internet.
6 If I'm going to be late, I always .... my parents from my mobile.

Revision key

Units 1 & 2

Unit 1

1 (Suggested answers)

1 How does your best friend go to school? He/She goes to school by car.

2 How many brothers and sisters have you got? I've got one sister.

3 What time does school finish? It finishes at half past four.

4 When do you do your homework? I do my homework when I get home.

5 Where do you and your friends go after school? We go to the park.

6 Who is your favourite cousin? My favourite cousin is Marco.

7 How do you go to the town centre? I walk to the town centre.

8 Where do you have lunch on a school day? I have lunch at school.

2 1 walk   2 start   3 have   4 get   5 do   6 watch   7 go

Unit 2

1 1 My mum often takes photographs of us.

2 We never sleep in a tent.

3 I'm sometimes late for my drawing classes.

4 I go to the cinema with my friends twice a month.

5 My friends do after-school activities every day.

6 My best friend often draws pictures.

2 1 collecting   2 drawing   3 taking   4 sleeping
5 watching   6 listening   7 going   8 writing

Units 3 & 4

Unit 3

1 1 is   2 a   3 an   4 are   5 any (or enough)   6 some

2 (Suggested answers)

1 I always have to do a lot of homework.

2 I don't have to wear a school uniform. I can wear what I like.

3 I don't have to make my breakfast. My dad makes it.

4 I have to work hard at school.

5 I don't have to get up early for school. I get up at eight o'clock.

6 I have to go to bed early on a school day.

3 1 cupboard   2 mirror   3 lamp   4 sofa   5 desk   6 bed
7 fridge   8 cooker

Unit 4

1 1 don't understand   2 don't go   3 watches
4 isn't raining   5 's winning   6 never wears
7 's studying   8 is that boy wearing

2 1 trainers   2 costume   3 helmet   4 socks   5 jeans
6 sweater

Units 5 & 6

Unit 5

1 1 was; on   2 didn't play; at   3 Did ... do; at
4 weren't; at   5 opened; on   6 Did ... have; in
7 didn't work; in   8 began; in

2 1 library   2 theatre   3 sports centre   4 museum
5 department store   6 newsagent   7 university
8 bookshop

Unit 6

1 (Suggested answers)

1 My dad's car isn't slower than my uncle's car.

2 My school isn't the biggest school in my town.

3 The countryside is more beautiful than the town.

4 Trains aren't more comfortable than planes.

5 Science is easier than maths.

6 The car isn't the worst transport in the world.

7 The school library isn't quieter than the library in my town.

8 My city isn't the largest city in my country.

2 1 ride   2 on   3 plane   4 sail   5 crossing   6 drive
7 by   8 bridges

Units 7 & 8

1 **1** can't **2** must **3** mustn't **4** shouldn't **5** can **6** can't **7** couldn't **8** could

2 **2** g **3** f **4** a **5** c **6** e **7** d

1 (Suggested answers)

1 Were your classmates speaking English at 11 a.m. yesterday? No, they weren't. They were studying maths.

2 Were you having a rest at 3 p.m. on Sunday? No, I wasn't. I was watching TV.

3 Were your friends and you talking when the class started? Yes, we were.

4 Were you sleeping last night at 11 p.m.? Yes, I was.

5 Was your dad making breakfast when you woke up this morning? No, he wasn't. He was having breakfast when I woke up.

6 Was it raining when you left home this morning? No, it wasn't. It was sunny.

7 Were you having lunch at 2 p.m. yesterday? Yes, I was.

2 **1** a rest **2** new dishes **3** on a campsite **4** the Amazon rainforest **5** many different languages **6** capital cities

Units 9 & 10

1 **1** We're (are) going to ride; Are you going to ask

2 I'm (am) going to play; I'm (am) not going to do; I'm (am) going to have

3 's (is) going to play; Is he going to play

4 We're (are) going to watch; I'm (am) going to study

5 isn't (is not) going to rain

2 **1** guitarist **2** actor **3** dancer **4** artist **5** photographer **6** drummer

1 **1** won't **2** may **3** will **4** may **5** will **6** will

2 **1** If the water is cold, I won't (will not) go swimming.

2 I'll (will) read a book if I don't (do not) go swimming.

3 If I finish the book, I'll (will) talk to my sister.

4 I'll (will) listen to music if my sister doesn't (does not) want to talk.

5 If I don't (do not) have my MP3 player, I'll (will) go for a walk.

3 **1** field **2** gate **3** wood **4** path **5** river **6** hill

Units 11 & 12

1 **1** 've (have) already visited **2** haven't (have not) brushed **3** Have you seen **4** 've (have) known **5** hasn't (has not) arrived

2 **1** yet **2** yet **3** just **4** yet **5** already **6** yet

3 **2** f **3** a **4** h **5** g **6** c **7** b **8** e

1 **1** My shoes are made of leather.

2 I'm (am) given money for my birthday.

3 Rugby isn't (is not) played at my school.

4 English is spoken all over the world.

5 CDs aren't sold here anymore.

2 **1** This book was written by my uncle.

2 My mum was taught how to cook at school.

3 We were told an interesting story this morning.

4 I was driven to school yesterday.

5 My friends weren't (were not) invited to the party.

3 **1** send **2** use **3** chat **4** play **5** download **6** call

Progress test 1 Units 1–4

1 Complete this conversation with the correct form of the verb in brackets. Use the present simple.

Tom: You look tired Megan. What time ....do........ you ...wake up... every morning?

Megan: About 7.30 but my brother (1) .... (wake up) at 6.30.

Tom: Why's that? What time (2) .... his school .... (start)?

Megan: It (3) .... (start) at 8.00.

Tom: That's early! (4) .... you .... (have got) a large family, Megan?

Megan: Just one brother but my dad (5) .... (have got) three sisters and four brothers.

Tom: Wow! That's big! I (6) .... (not have got) any brothers or sisters.

Megan: Really? What about your school? How (7) .... you .... (go) to school?

Tom: I (8) .... (walk) there with my friends.

Megan: (9) .... you and your friends .... (have) lunch at school?

Tom: Yes, we do. Then after lunch, we (10) .... (play) football in the playground.

Megan: I (11) .... (not play) games at lunchtime. I (12) .... (do) my homework in the school library.

2 Circle the best word to complete each sentence.

My uncle's wife is my *dad* / *mum* / (*aunt*.)

1 Your dad's brother is your *uncle* / *cousin* / *aunt*.

2 Your mum and your dad are your *parents* / *children* / *fathers*.

3 Before I watch TV, I *do* / *make* / *write* my homework.

4 At the weekends, I *get* / *go* / *make* to bed at 11 o'clock.

5 What time is it? I haven't got a *towel* / *diary* / *watch*.

6 My best friend's hair isn't straight – it's *long* / *curly* / *tall*.

7 Is that the new maths teacher? She's very *tall* / *long* / *curly*.

8 A: What does your brother *like* / *look* / *look like*?
B: He's tall with green eyes.

3 Read the question and write a complete answer. Use the word or expression in brackets.

How often do you go to the cinema? (twice a month)
.....*I go to the cinema twice a month.*..................

1 How often does your teacher give you homework? (every day).

....

2 How often do you and your friends play tennis? (sometimes)

....

3 How often does your mum have lunch at home? (usually)

....

4 How often do your grandparents phone you? (once a day)

....

5 How often are you late for school? (never)

....

6 How often do you get up before eight o'clock? (always)

....

4 Match the sentence beginnings (1–8) with the sentence ends (a–h) [line joining 1 and d]

1 On holiday, I often take   a a film every weekend.

2 My brother loves collecting

3 My family watches   b the violin in a band with my friends.

4 I always listen to

5 My aunt is brilliant at drawing   c in a tent when it rains.

6 I'm sure my friends play   d photos of my family.

7 Once a week, I play   e music when I study.

8 I really don't like sleeping   f things. He's got 1,000 bus tickets.

      g pictures of animals. She's very clever.

      h sports every day. They love sport.

5 Choose the best answer (A, B or C) for each space.

How .... beds are there in your bedroom?
(A) many   B much   C any

1 How .... bread do you eat every day?
   A much   B many   C few

2 There isn't .... milk in the fridge.
   A some   B one   C any

3 .... there a sofa in your bedroom?
   A Is   B Are   C Do

4 We eat a .... of vegetables in my house.
   A few   B little   C lot

5 Can I have a .... jam, please?
   A few   B little   C lot

6 Are there .... flowers in your aunt's garden?
   A few   B much   C any

7 Have you got .... oil?
   A any   B a   C an

8 Don't put .... tomatoes in the salad.
   A some   B any   C a

6 Complete these sentences with the words in the box.

cooker lamp sofa fridge mirror chairs
desk cupboard bed

Don't touch the ......cooker...... ! It's still very hot.

1 Do you sit at a .... in your bedroom when you study?
2 I can't see. Can you turn on the ...., please?
3 After dinner, we sit together on the .... in the living-room and watch TV.
4 I always brush my hair in front of the .... so I can see myself.
5 I think there's some cold water in the ....
6 All the plates are in the .... next to the fridge.
7 My sister spends hours lying on her .... in her bedroom.
8 We usually have dinner in the kitchen because there's a table and four ....

7 Complete the sentences with the correct form of the verb in brackets. Use the present simple or the present continuous.

She never ......does...... (do) athletics.

1 Kevin .... (not win) the match at the moment.
2 We sometimes .... (play) basketball on Saturday afternoon.
3 Why .... Jenny .... (carry) three tennis rackets right now?
4 My best friend .... (not come) from England.
5 How often .... you .... (go) swimming after school?
6 Look! Jacob and Pete .... (wear) the same trainers today.
7 I .... (hope) to win a race soon.
8 I .... (study) history because we've got a test tomorrow.

8 Complete these sentences with go, play or do and a sport from the box.

fishing football ice-skating skateboarding
athletics skiing tennis surfing swimming

I often ..go..fishing. with my uncle. We sit next to the river but we never catch anything.

1 Put on your skates and let's ....
2 I want to .... but my brother's using my surfboard.
3 Would you like to .... ? I've got two rackets and some balls.
4 When it snows, my cousins usually .... in the mountains.
5 Can I borrow your swimming costume? I'd like to .... in the pool later.
6 Do you want to .... at the new skate park?
7 On Sunday morning, my friends and I take a ball to the park and we ....
8 I .... twice a week after school. My favourite thing is running.

Progress test 2 Units 5–8

1 Complete these sentences with the past simple positive or negative form of these verbs.

> ~~go~~ have buy be study enjoy watch
> do drink

My friends ......_went_...... to the police station on their school trip.

1 We .... a great time at the museum yesterday.

2 You were thirsty yesterday because you .... (not) anything all day.

3 I .... these new trainers at the department store two days ago.

4 We .... a great film at the cinema last Saturday.

5 I .... (not) my homework yesterday because I was tired.

6 There .... a lot of people at the theatre last night.

7 It was very noisy in the kitchen so I .... for the history test in my bedroom.

8 We .... ourselves at Nick's party on Saturday.

2 Complete these sentences with the words in the box.

> police station university theatre cinema
> museum bookshop department store
> newsagent

My dad's a police officer. He works in the ...._police station_.... in my town.

1 The .... in our town sells everything from clothes to musical instruments.

2 My cousin's studying history at the .... in my town.

3 Can you go to the .... and buy me a newspaper, please?

4 We saw a great exhibition about time machines at the Science ....

5 There's a comedy film on at the .... on Saturday.

6 This company sells books all over the world. It's the largest online .... in the world.

7 Our teacher took us to the .... to see a funny play.

3 Choose the best word to complete the sentences.

Trains are (faster)/ fastest than cars.

1 Travelling by plane is more / most expensive than travelling by bus.

2 Madrid is the largest / larger city in my country.

3 I think the football museum is the better / best museum in the world.

4 Watching a film at home is cheaper / cheapest than going to the cinema.

5 The market car park is bigger / biggest than the car park under the department store.

6 This is the busier / busiest roundabout in my town.

7 The Chinese Theater in Hollywood is one of the more / most famous cinemas in the world.

8 Playing sport is more / most interesting than watching it.

4 Read the description and write the word.

This is to travel by plane.
f _l_ _y_

1 You need to walk over this to cross the river.
b _ _ _ _ _

2 When these are red, you have to stop.
t _ _ _ _ _ _ _ l _ _ _ _ _

3 You can swim, play basketball or do aerobics in this place.
s _ _ _ _ _ c _ _ _ _ _

4 This is to travel by ship or boat.
s _ _ _

5 If you go cycling, you do this with your bike.
r _ _ _

6 This comfortable bus takes you on long journeys.
c _ _ _ _

7 This is a type of train that travels on the road.
t _ _ _

8 You do this if you go on foot.
w _ _ _

5 **Choose the best answer (A, B or C) for each space.**

No running inside the school. You .... walk.

A could   (B) must   C can

1 When my mum was young, she .... play the violin really well.

A could   B must   C should

2 No food or drink at all times! You .... eat or drink in class.

A shouldn't   B mustn't   C couldn't

3 If you want to pass the exam, you .... study a little more.

A could   B can   C should

4 Please speak more loudly. We .... hear you.

A can't   B mustn't   C shouldn't

5 My dad .... swim until he was ten years old because he didn't live near a swimming pool.

A couldn't   B mustn't   C can't

6 My sister's good at athletics. She .... run really fast.

A must   B could   C can

7 I'm sorry I .... come to your party last week. I was ill.

A couldn't   B can't   C shouldn't

8 You .... worry so much about the test. You'll be fine.

A couldn't   B shouldn't   C can't

6 **Choose the best word to complete the sentence.**

I often get worried before I *pass* / (*take*) an exam.

1 I *learnt* / *studied* how to ride a bike when I was five.

2 I *missed* / *lost* a class because I was at the dentist.

3 She didn't work hard so she *failed* / *passed* the exam.

4 In our geography class, we're *teaching* / *learning* about the weather.

5 I often *use* / *spend* hours listening to music.

6 My aunt is a teacher. She *teaches* / *learns* us maths at our school.

7 **Complete the sentences with the correct form of the verbs. Use the past simple or past continuous.**

It ..*wasn't raining*.. (not rain) when I woke up this morning.

1 When we got to the top of the mountain, we .... (have) a rest.

2 We .... (not talk) loudly when our teacher came into the class.

3 She was climbing a tree when she .... (fall) and broke her arm.

4 I was listening to music while I .... (do) my homework.

5 Our teacher .... (not leave) the classroom while we were doing the test.

6 While we were exploring the city, we .... (find) a café which sold brilliant ice cream.

7 I .... (stay) in Tokyo when I tried Japanese food for the first time.

8 While my dad was learning German in Berlin, he .... (meet) my mum.

8 **Choose the best answer (a or b).**

I didn't watch the end of the film because ...

    (a) it was boring.
    b it was amazing.

1 It took us 11 hours to get home and then I went to bed.

    a The journey was funny.
    b The journey was tiring.

2 I want to go back to New York again.

    a It's a terrible city.
    b It's a wonderful city.

3 I laughed and laughed.

    a The film was funny.
    b The film was boring.

4 We didn't like the food in that restaurant at all.

    a It was terrible.
    b It was amazing.

5 We all had a great time at the museum.

    a It was very interesting.
    b It was very boring.

6 You've got 95% in the test.

    a That's terrible!
    b That's excellent!

Progress test 3 Units 9–12

1 Write complete sentences. Use *be going to*: positive or negative.

(I/watch a film)
...... I'm going to watch a film. ......

1 (My brother / study / in Canada)

....

2 (We / see / the new photography exhibition)

....

3 (I / not have lunch / at school today)

....

4 (My friends / not ride / their bikes later)

....

5 (You / enjoy / the circus)

....

6 (My aunt / stay / with us for five days)

....

7 (It / not be / sunny in the afternoon)

....

8 (Our teachers / sing / in the concert)

....

2 Use a form of the words in capitals to complete each sentence.

My dad works for a newspaper.
He's a journalist .   JOURNAL

1 I love taking photos. I want
to be a .... when I'm   PHOTOGRAPH
older.

2 The musicians are very good
but the .... is amazing.   SING

3 My favourite .... is   ART
Picasso. I love his pictures.

4 My sisters hopes to be a
.... She really enjoys   WRITE
writing stories.

5 My brother's a brilliant
.... He plays in a band.   GUITAR

6 I'm terrible at singing and I'm
not a very good ....   DANCE

7 I would like to be a famous
.... and work in a theatre.   ACT

8 That .... is playing very   DRUM
loudly. I can't hear anything.

3 Complete the sentences with the correct form of the verb in brackets. Use the first conditional.

If we ...... follow ...... (follow) this path, we ...... 'll get ...... (get)
to Jacob's Farm.

1 If we .... (get) lost, we .... (phone) my
dad.

2 I .... (not go) to the lake, if it .... (rain)
tomorrow.

3 If we .... (not do) our homework, our teacher
.... (not be) pleased.

4 If they .... (take) the train at nine o'clock, they
.... (arrive) here before 10.30.

5 He .... (get) wet if he .... (not wear) a
coat.

6 If you .... (eat) that sandwich now, you
.... (not be) hungry later.

7 It .... (be) quicker if we .... (go) over
that bridge.

8 If the cows .... (not be) in that field, I
.... (walk) across it.

4 Complete the email with the words in the box.

farm   rain   clouds   path   wind   lake   gate
field   hill

From: Rob

To: Neil

We're having a great time at Tresson ...... farm .... Today, there
are a lot of (1) .... in the sky. It may (2) ....
later but we're going for a walk. We're going to walk across the
(3) .... where the horses are again. Last time I forgot
to close the (4) .... and the farmer got angry. Then,
we're going to take the (5) .... which goes up the
(6) .... At the top, you see the (7) .... with
small boats on it. My dad says if there's a lot of (8) ....
up there, it'll be very cold.

Compact Key for Schools by Emma Heyderman © Cambridge University Press 2014   **Photocopiable**

5 Choose the best answer (A, B or C) for each space.

Have you brushed your teeth _____ ?
A just   (B) yet   C already

1 Ow! I've _____ cut my foot and it hurts.
A yet   B just   C since

2 We've _____ seen that film three times. Can we watch something else?
A already   B since   C yet

3 I've known my best friend _____ three years.
A already   B for   C since

4 My friends haven't won a match _____ January.
A for   B just   C since

5 I've had a terrible cold _____ Saturday.
A since   B for   C ago

6 Our maths teacher hasn't arrived _____ . That's strange.
A just   B already   C yet

6 Complete the sentences with the words in the box.

| hurts well burnt toothache cut down |
| temperature broken matter |

I've just finished football practice and my back _____hurts_____ a lot.

1 Can I go home? I don't feel _____ .

2 You look terrible. What's the _____ ?

3 Mum! Karen's just _____ her hand on the cooker.

4 Ow! I've just hurt my arm. I think it may be _____ .

5 You're very hot. I think you've got a _____ .

6 I'm going to lie _____ . My head hurts and I feel ill.

7 Our teacher's had _____ since last week but he hasn't been to the dentist yet.

8 She's just broken a glass and _____ her hand. I'll clean it and put a plaster on it.

7 Choose the best verb to complete the sentences.

My grandma are often given / (is often given) flowers for her birthday.

1 I 'm called / 're called Blue by my friends because I've got a blue bike.

2 Tickets for the concert aren't sold / isn't sold here.

3 The window wasn't broken / weren't broken by those boys.

4 My shoes was made / were made in India.

5 We 're driven / were driven to school every day at 7.30. School starts at eight o'clock.

6 I am taught / was taught how to ride a bike when I was five years old.

7 The Internet uses / 's used all over the world.

8 Many people download / are downloaded films from this website.

8 Read the description and write the word.

People often listen to music on this.
M P 3   p l a y e r

1 You look at the words and pictures on this part of the computer.
s _ _ _ _ _

2 This is used to take photos.
c _ _ _ _ _

3 This is a small computer which you can carry.
l _ _ _ _ _

4 You do this to get music, films or pictures from the Internet.
d _ _ _ _ _ _ _

5 If you send a message on your phone, you do this.
t _ _ _

6 This is another word for 'to phone'.
c _ _ _

7 You click on this to change things on the computer.
m _ _ _ _

8 You need this if you want to send a message to someone on the computer.
e _ _ _ _   a _ _ _ _ _ _

Progress tests key

Progress Test Units 1–4

1 1 wakes up   2 does … start   3 starts   4 Have … got
5 's (has) got   6 haven't (have not) got   7 do … go
8 walk   9 Do … have   10 play   11 don't (do not) play
12 do

2 1 uncle   2 parents   3 do   4 go   5 watch   6 curly
7 tall   8 look like

3 1 My teacher / He / She gives us homework every day.
2 My friends and I / We sometimes play tennis.
3 My mum / She usually has lunch at home.
4 My grandparents / They phone me once a day.
5 I'm (am) never late for school.
6 I always get up before eight o'clock.

4 2 f   3 a   4 e   5 g   6 h   7 b   8 c

5 1 A   2 C   3 A   4 C   5 B   6 C   7 A   8 B

6 1 desk   2 lamp   3 sofa   4 mirror   5 fridge
6 cupboard   7 bed   8 chairs

7 1 isn't (is not) winning   2 play   3 is … carrying
4 doesn't (does not) come   5 do … go   6 are wearing
7 hope / am hoping   8 'm (am) studying

8 1 go ice-skating   2 go surfing   3 play tennis
4 go skiing   5 go swimming   6 go skateboarding
7 play football   8 do athletics

Progress Test 2 Units 5–8

1 1 had   2 didn't drink   3 bought   4 watched
5 didn't do   6 were   7 studied   8 enjoyed

2 1 department store   2 university   3 newsagent
4 museum   5 cinema   6 bookshop   7 theatre

3 1 more   2 largest   3 best   4 cheaper   5 bigger
6 busiest   7 most   8 more

4 1 bridge   2 traffic lights   3 sports centre   4 sail
5 ride   6 coach   7 tram   8 walk

5 1 A   2 B   3 C   4 A   5 A   6 C   7 A   8 B

6 1 learnt   2 missed   3 failed   4 learning   5 spend
6 teaches

7 1 had   2 weren't (were not) talking   3 fell
4 was doing / did   5 didn't (did not) leave   6 found
7 was staying   8 met

8 1 b   2 b   3 a   4 a   5 a   6 b

Progress Test 3 Units 9–12

1 1 My brother's (is) going to study in Canada.
2 We're (are) going to see the new photography
exhibition.
3 I'm (am) not going to have lunch at school today.
4 My friends aren't (are not) going to ride their bikes
later.
5 You're (are) going to enjoy the circus.
6 My aunt's (is) going to stay/ with us for five days.
7 It isn't (is not) going to be sunny in the afternoon.
8 Our teachers are going to sing in the concert.

2 1 photographer   2 singer   3 artist   4 writer
5 guitarist   6 dancer   7 actor   8 drummer

3 1 get; 'll (will) phone   2 won't (will not) go; rains
3 don't (do not) do; won't (will not) be pleased
4 take; 'll (will) arrive   5 'll (will) get; doesn't (does
not) wear   6 eat, won't (will not) be   7 'll (will) be; go
8 aren't (are not); 'll (will) walk

4 1 clouds   2 rain   3 field   4 gate   5 path   6 hill
7 lake   8 wind

5 1 B   2 A   3 B   4 C   5 A   6 C

6 1 well   2 matter   3 burnt   4 broken   5 temperature
6 down   7 toothache   8 cut

7 1 'm called   2 aren't sold   3 wasn't broken
4 were made   5 're driven   6 was taught   7 's used
8 download

8 1 screen   2 camera   3 laptop   4 download   5 text
6 call   7 mouse   8 email address

Practice test key & script

A further practice test is available at www.cambridge.org/compactkeyforschools

Reading and Writing

Part 1
1 C 2 E 3 F 4 H 5 D

Part 2
6 C 7 C 8 A 9 B 10 A

Part 3
11 C 12 B 13 B 14 A 15 B
16 H 17 G 18 B 19 D 20 A

Part 4
21 A 22 C 23 A 24 B 25 B 26 A 27 B

Part 5
28 C 29 B 30 C 31 A 32 C 33 C 34 B 35 C

Part 6
36 bird 37 tree 38 gate 39 clouds 40 grass

Part 7
41 are 42 the 43 this 44 from 45 than 46 has
47 about 48 not 49 it 50 Do

Part 8
51 Jack Bond 52 0777 562398 53 blue 54 (£) 62.50
55 age

Listening

Part 1
1 C 2 B 3 A 4 B 5 A

Part 2
6 Kate – A 7 Anna – H 8 Eric – C 9 Leo – D
10 Jade – B

Part 3
11 B 12 C 13 A 14 C 15 B

Part 4
16 Rowdle 17 6 / six 18 towel 19 singing
20 £11.50 /eleven pounds fifty (pence)

Part 5
21 Market 22 (a / the) cinema 23 £19.75 / nineteen pounds
seventy-five 24 Thursday(s) 25 shocalit

Part 1 🔊 44

Look at the instructions for Part One.	
Narrator:	*You will hear five short conversations.*
	You will hear each conversation twice.
	There is one question for each conversation.
	For each question, choose the right answer (A, B or C).
	Here is an example:
	How will the boy get to Ben's house?
Boy:	Mum can you drive me to Ben's house this morning?
Mum:	No, because Dad's got the car. Why can't you walk?
Boy:	Because it's going to rain – look at the clouds! I'll take the bus. It stops near Ben's house.
Mum:	OK.
Narrator:	*The answer is B. Now we are ready to start.*
One	*How will the girl's mother pay for the CD?*
Girl:	Can I have this CD, please?
Man:	OK. Are you paying with cash?
Girl:	My mum's going to pay – she's coming now. But will you take a cheque? She's forgotten her credit card.
Man:	Of course.
Now listen again.	
Two	*What time does Marley's café close?*
Girl:	My friends and I are going to Marley's café after tennis club, Dad.
Man:	But it closes at five o'clock. You won't have much time there.
Girl:	No, it's changed. It's open until seven, now. But I'll be home at about six, I think.
Man:	All right, that's fine.
Now listen again.	
Three	*Where will they have their picnic?*
Boy:	We can sit by the river for our picnic, Dad. Look, there's a nice place on the grass.
Man:	It's too wet. How about on that big rock by the tree?
Boy:	Yeah, OK. But can we go in the boat before we have the picnic?
Man:	Come on then.
Now listen again.	
Four	*What is too small for the girl?*
Woman:	Is that your T-shirt from Grandma? It looks really nice on you.
Girl:	Yes, it's just right. But the skirt she gave me isn't big enough. I'll have to ask her to change it.
Woman:	What about the hat Grandma gave you?
Girl:	It's quite large on me, but I like it.

Now listen again.

Five	*What does Donna want for dinner?*
Man:	I'm cooking fish for dinner, Donna. Do you want potatoes with it?
Girl:	Er ... could we have pasta? We haven't had that for ages.
Man:	Of course. I'm glad you didn't ask for rice – we haven't got any!
Girl:	Can we have a bit of salad, too?

Now listen again. That is the end of Part One.

Part 2 🎧 45

Narrator: Listen to Sandi talking to her mum about snacks.

What snacks do her friends want?

For questions 6–10, write a letter A–H next to each person.

You will hear the conversation twice.

Woman:	Sandi, have you asked your friends what snacks they want before you all go to the cinema?
Girl:	Yes, I wrote it down!
Woman:	Great! First, you, Sandi – I guess you want some banana cake?
Girl:	Of course! A big piece, please!
Woman:	Right. Who else wants cake?
Girl:	No one. Some of them want fruit ... Kate does. She's just had some chocolate so she wants a nice healthy apple now – that green one looks nice.
Woman:	OK. What about Anna? She always has cheese, doesn't she?
Girl:	She loves cheese, but she's asked for an orange today.
Woman:	Right. Does Eric want fruit, too?
Girl:	He wants some bread and butter. He's really hungry because he only had a few biscuits for his lunch.
Woman:	OK. I'll cut two slices for him. What about Eric's friend, Leo?
Girl:	He'd like some biscuits, but the ones without chocolate in them.
Woman:	OK. So there's only one more person: Jade.
Girl:	Yes, she asked for a banana if we've got one, or an apple if not.
Woman:	We *have* got one, here it is. I've put everything on two big plates. Shall I help you carry them into the living room?
Girl:	Thanks, Mum.

Now listen again.

That is the end of Part Two.

Part 3 🎧 46

Narrator: Now look at Part Three.

Listen to Ahmet talking to his friend Lizzie about football and swimming.

For each question choose the right answer (A, B or C).

You will hear the conversation twice.

Look at questions 11–15 now. You have twenty seconds.

Now listen to the conversation.

Girl:	How was the football match you went to see on Saturday, Ahmet?
Boy:	Not bad, thanks, Lizzie. It was a great game but my team lost, 2–1. They played very well, though.
Girl:	So what happened, why didn't they win then?
Boy:	Well, our best player scored the goal after only ten minutes. But he only played for twenty minutes because he fell and hurt his foot. So the seventy minutes after that were difficult for the team.
Girl:	Yes. Did you go to the match with your dad and your sister?
Boy:	That's right. My sister never misses a match. She knows more about the team than we do now.
Girl:	Really? Does your sister *play* football, too?
Boy:	Yes, she does. She's in quite a good girls' team.
Girl:	Which one? My cousin plays for the East Side team – is that the same one?
Boy:	No, my sister's is called King's Park. Their club's in Old Town. But she's played matches against East Side before. Maybe she knows your cousin.
Girl:	Perhaps. You don't play football, do you Ahmet? You're a swimmer.
Boy:	I am. I have swimming practice three times a week, and I study the other two week-day nights – I've got exams soon. So I don't have any evenings free to play football.
Girl:	Right. Are you going swimming now?
Boy:	Not now. First, I'm going to the library to get some books, and then I'm going home for dinner. I'll go to the pool after that.
Girl:	OK. See you soon!

Narrator: Now listen again.

This is the end of Part Three.

Part 4 🎧 47

Narrator: Now look at Part Four.

You will hear a mother and son talking about a surf camp.

Listen and complete each question.

You will hear the conversation twice.

Woman:	Billy? I want to tell you about your surf camp.
Boy:	Oh yes. When is it?
Woman:	In August, for three days, the 11th to the 13th.
Boy:	OK. And the camp's by the sea – but near which beach?
Woman:	It's not far from Rowdle Beach.

Boy:	What? How do you spell that, Mum? I want to look at it online.
Woman:	R–O–W–D–L–E. And that's where your lessons will be.
Boy:	OK. Will I be in a big class?
Woman:	No, in yours, Class 10, there'll be just six of you learning to surf, with two teachers.
Boy:	Great. And what do I need to take to lessons?
Woman:	Just a towel. You wear your swimming costume, of course. And Surf Camp gives you the board.
Boy:	Brilliant. And what happens in the evenings?
Woman:	Games on the beach and singing. You can choose which activity to do.
Boy:	Sounds good. Anything else?
Woman:	Yes, you can get nice surf camp bags – they're £11.50, or sweatshirts for £9.50. You need a new bag.
Boy:	Yes, can you get me one, please?
Woman:	OK.
Narrator:	Now listen again.
	This is the end of Part Four.

Part 5 48

Narrator:	Now look at Part Five.
	You will hear an advertisement for a new clothes shop.
	Listen and complete each question.
	You will hear the information twice.
	If you're a teenager who loves clothes, then this is the shop for you! The name of our new shop is Sweet Stuff and we're in the centre of the town. Our shop is in Market Street, the best place to get all the newest fashions. You can't miss it, it's the big shop opposite the park, right next to the cinema. For this week only, we're selling boys' jeans at the amazing price of nineteen pounds seventy-five! That's about ten pounds cheaper than anywhere else! We're open Monday to Saturday from nine o'clock and you can come and shop until eight on Thursdays! The other days we close at six. If you want to have a look at the clothes we sell, why not visit our website? You can also order clothes on the site and collect them from the shop. The address is www.shocalit.com, that's www.S–H–O–C–A–L–I–T.com. See you soon!
Narrator:	Now listen again.
	This is the end of Part Five.

Sample answer sheets

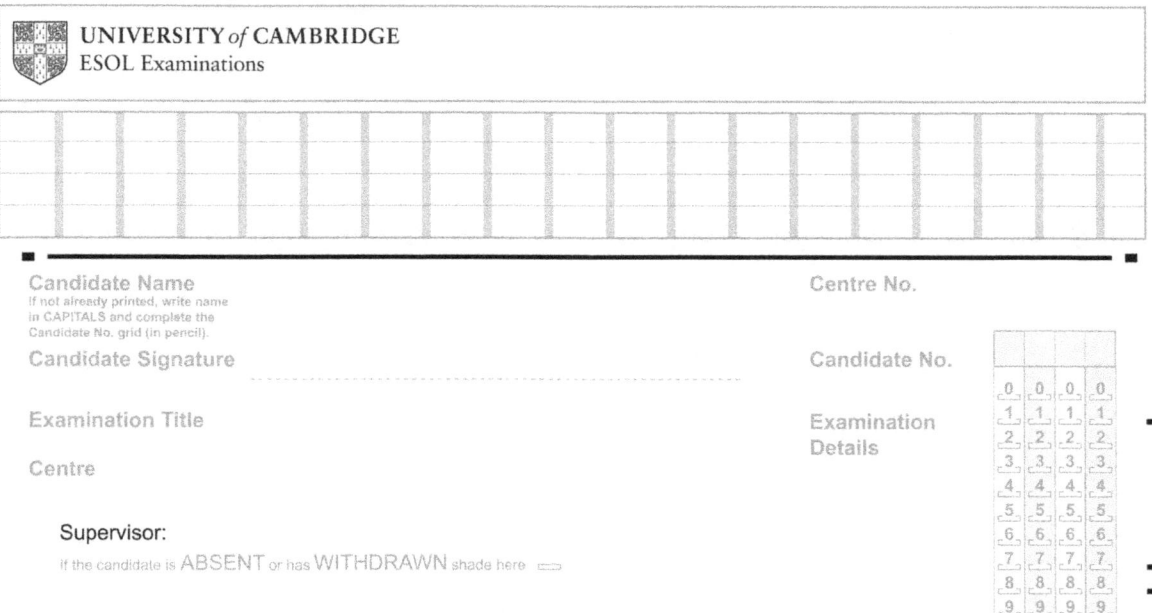

UNIVERSITY *of* **CAMBRIDGE**
ESOL Examinations

Candidate Name
If not already printed, write name
in CAPITALS and complete the
Candidate No. grid (in pencil).

Centre No.

Candidate Signature

Candidate No.

Examination Title

Examination
Details

Centre

Supervisor:
If the candidate is ABSENT or has WITHDRAWN shade here ⊂⊃

KET Paper 1 Reading and Writing Candidate Answer Sheet

Instructions

Use a PENCIL (B or HB).
Rub out any answer you want to change with an eraser.

For **Parts 1, 2, 3, 4** and **5**:
Mark ONE letter for each question.
For example, if you think **C** is the right answer to the
question, mark your answer sheet like this:

0	A B C

Part 1

1	A B C D E F G H
2	A B C D E F G H
3	A B C D E F G H
4	A B C D E F G H
5	A B C D E F G H

Part 2

6	A B C
7	A B C
8	A B C
9	A B C
10	A B C

Part 3

11	A B C
12	A B C
13	A B C
14	A B C
15	A B C

16	A B C D E F G H
17	A B C D E F G H
18	A B C D E F G H
19	A B C D E F G H
20	A B C D E F G H

Part 4

21	A B C
22	A B C
23	A B C
24	A B C
25	A B C
26	A B C
27	A B C

Part 5

28	A B C
29	A B C
30	A B C
31	A B C
32	A B C
33	A B C
34	A B C
35	A B C

Turn over for
Parts 6 - 9 →

Sample answer sheets

For **Parts 6, 7 and 8:**

Write your answers in the spaces next to the numbers (36 to 55) like this:

0	example

Part 6		Do not write here
36		1 36 0
37		1 37 0
38		1 38 0
39		1 39 0
40		1 40 0

Part 7		Do not write here
41		1 41 0
42		1 42 0
43		1 43 0
44		1 44 0
45		1 45 0
46		1 46 0
47		1 47 0
48		1 48 0
49		1 49 0
50		1 50 0

Part 8		Do not write here
51		1 51 0
52		1 52 0
53		1 53 0
54		1 54 0
55		1 55 0

Part 9 (Question 56): Write your answer below.

Do not write below (Examiner use only)					
0	1	2	3	4	5

Sample answer sheets

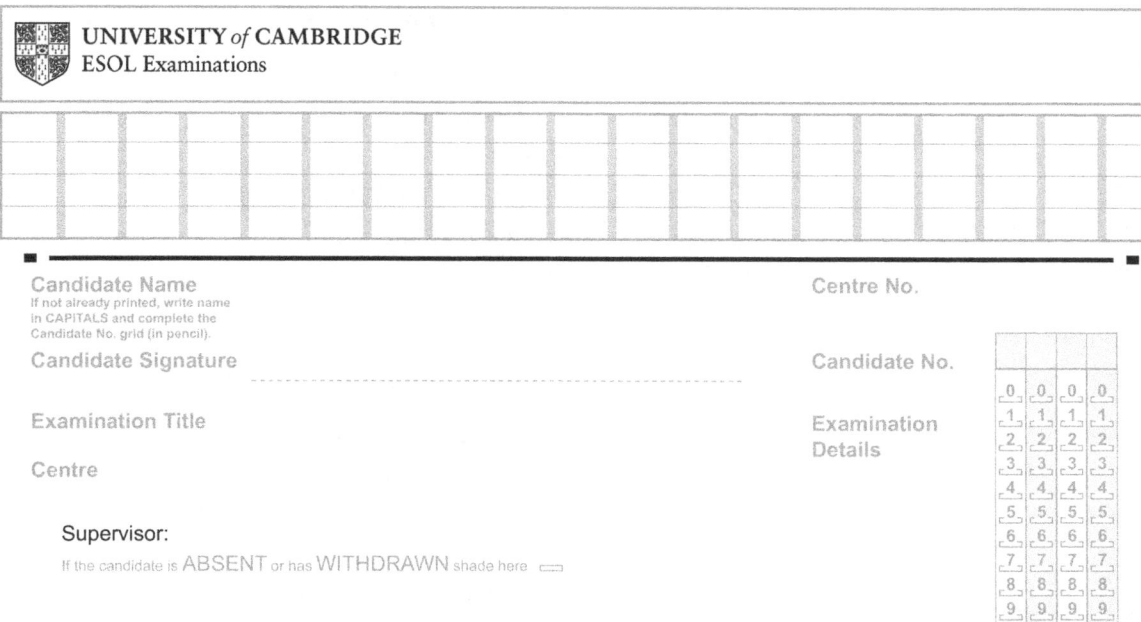

UNIVERSITY *of* **CAMBRIDGE**
ESOL Examinations

Candidate Name
If not already printed, write name
in CAPITALS and complete the
Candidate No. grid (in pencil).

Candidate Signature

Examination Title

Centre

Supervisor:

If the candidate is ABSENT or has WITHDRAWN shade here ▭

Centre No.

Candidate No.

Examination
Details

KET Paper 2 Listening Candidate Answer Sheet

Instructions

Use a PENCIL (B or HB).

Rub out any answer you want to change with an eraser.

For **Parts 1, 2** and **3**:
Mark ONE letter for each question.
For example, if you think **C** is the right answer to the
question, mark your answer sheet like this:

Part 1			
1	A	B	C
2	A	B	C
3	A	B	C
4	A	B	C
5	A	B	C

Part 2								
6	A	B	C	D	E	F	G	H
7	A	B	C	D	E	F	G	H
8	A	B	C	D	E	F	G	H
9	A	B	C	D	E	F	G	H
10	A	B	C	D	E	F	G	H

Part 3			
11	A	B	C
12	A	B	C
13	A	B	C
14	A	B	C
15	A	B	C

For **Parts 4** and **5**:
Write your answers in the spaces next to the
numbers (16 to 25) like this:

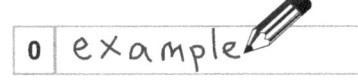

Part 4	Do not write here
16	1 16 0
17	1 17 0
18	1 18 0
19	1 19 0
20	1 20 0

Part 5	Do not write here
21	1 21 0
22	1 22 0
23	1 23 0
24	1 24 0
25	1 25 0

Speaking guide key

1 2 personal information   3 the students   4 words

2 2 should   3 shouldn't   4 should   5 shouldn't   6 shouldn't

Part 1

1 (Suggested answers)
2 It's Hansen.   3 It's H-A-N-S-E-N.

2 (Suggested answers)
2 I live in Pisa in Italy.   3 Yes, I study English at school.
4 I also study maths, history, science and sport.
5 I like maths best because I'm good at it.   6 I like my school because I've got a lot of friends there and the teachers are very good.

3 2 a   3 b   4 e   5 f   6 d

4 (Suggested answers)
2 At the weekend, I'm going to watch a film with my friends on Saturday afternoon. After that, we're going to have pizza at my friend's house. On Sunday, I'm going to do my homework.
3 My favourite television programme is a quiz show. Three teams of people have to answer different questions and do different things. The winners get amazing prizes like a new TV or a lot of money.

Part 2: asking questions

1 2 Is   3 is   4 does   5 's (is)

2 2 What time does it open?   3 When is the first class?
4 Is it open every day?   5 What date is the show?
6 What time are the lessons?

3 2 a   3 b   4 e   5 d

4 2 What can we see there?   3 What can you learn?
4 What can I do there?   5 What can I read about?

Part 2: answering questions

1 2 They're (are)   3 They cost   4 No, it's   5 It's

2 (Suggested answers)
2 No, it's open Monday to Saturday. / No, it's closed on Sunday.
3 It closes at 5.00 p.m.
4 It's on sale from next week.
5 They're on Mondays and Fridays.
6 The concert's on 30th July.

3 (Suggested answers)
2 I live in Madrid, Spain.
3 It's 6713332.   4 It's jon@gmail.com
5 I like www.marca.com

4 2 d   3 e   4 a   5 b

Student A – Paper 3 Speaking

Part 1   (Suggested answers)

A: Good morning!

B: Good morning!

A: What's your name?

B: My name's Lucia.

A: What's your surname?

B: It's Pardo.

A: How do you spell it?

B: It's P-A-R-D-O.

A: Where do you come from?

B: I come from Spain.

A: Do you study English at school?

B: Yes, I do.

A: What other subjects do you study?

B: I study maths, Spanish, geography and science.

A: What subject do you like best?

B: I like science best.

A: Why?

B: Because the teacher is very good.

A: What's your favourite food?

B: I like pizza.

A: Who usually cooks in your house?

B: My mum usually cooks but my dad sometimes cooks, too.

A: What time did you have breakfast this morning?

B: I had breakfast at a quarter past seven this morning.

A: Tell me something about your best friend.

B: Her name's Sofia and she goes to my school. She's tall with long dark hair. She plays basketball very well and she's a good dancer, too.

Student B – Paper 3 Speaking

Part 1   (Suggested answers)

B: Good afternoon!

A: Good afternoon!

B: What's your name?

A: My name's Cristiano.

B: What's your surname?

A: My surname's Gomes.

B: How do you spell it?

A: It's G-O-M-E-S.

B: Where do you live?

A: I live in Porto in Portugal.

B: Do you study English at school?

A: Yes, I study English at school.

B: What other subjects do you study?

A: I study history, music, science and maths.

B: What do you like best about your school?

A: I have got a lot of friends at my school.

B: What do you usually do at the weekend?

A: I usually play football on Saturdays.

B: How often do you meet your friends?

A: I often meet my friends on Saturday afternoons.

B: What are you going to do this weekend?

A: I think I'm going to play football.

B: Tell me something about your family.

A: I've got a large family. I've got three brothers and a sister. My three brothers are older than me and my sister is younger than me. Her name is Carla and she goes to my school.

Part 2 (Suggested answers)

New cinema

B: When does the new cinema open?

A: It opens on 1st March.

B: Can I buy something to eat at the cinema?

A: Yes, you can buy cheap snacks and drinks in the shop.

B: How much are the tickets?

A: All the films are £6.

B: Where is the cinema?

A: It's in the Kings Shopping Centre.

B: How can I get more information?

B: You can visit www.filmworld.com

Guitar Lessons

A: Where are the guitar lessons?

B: They're at The Music Shop.

A: What's the name of the teacher?

B: The teacher's name is Matt.

A: When are the lessons?

B: They're at 11.00 a.m. on Saturdays.

A: How much do the lessons cost?

B: They are only £7 a lesson.

A: What's the phone number?

B: It's 751332.

Grammar reference key

Unit 1

1 2 Have you got a pet?

3 Has your neighbour got a mountain bike?

4 Have your classmates got a lot of free time?

5 Has your best friend got a favourite team?

6 Have you and your friends got a favourite place to meet?

2 2 My mum ~~cookes~~ = cooks   3 School ~~finises~~ = finishes
4 I ~~doun't~~ know = don't   5 The library ~~openes~~ = opens
6 I ~~lik~~ = like

Unit 2

1 1 I often draw pictures in class.

2 My brother never takes photographs of his friends.

3 I play tennis twice a week.

4 I am usually tired on Monday morning.

5 My friends listen to music every day.

6 My parents often watch a film after dinner.

2 1 going   2 Would; to come; love   3 Do; drawing
4 Does; making   5 Would   6 Do; playing

Unit 3

1 2 How many students are there in your class? There are a lot of students in my class.

3 How much hot chocolate is there in your cup? There isn't any hot chocolate in my cup.

4 How much time is there before this class ends? There's a lot of time before this class ends.

5 How many posters are there on your bedroom walls? There aren't any posters on my bedroom walls.

6 How much money is there in your pocket? There's a little money in my pocket.

7 How many books are there in your bedroom? There are a few books in my bedroom.

2 2 has to do   3 have to wash up   4 don't have to wear
5 doesn't have to help   6 have to wash
7 don't have to buy

Unit 4

2 'm (am) watching   3 spend   4 's (is) winning
5 Do; like   6 play   7 goes   8 are riding
9 'm (am) finishing

Unit 5

1 1 at   2 On   3 at   4 In   5 in   6 –   7 in   8 –   9 in
10 on

2 1 The museum opened on 23rd June, 1998.

2 My friends stayed at my house yesterday.

3 We took photos of the town in the morning.

4 I didn't go to football practice on my birthday.

5 It rained a lot in March.

6 My teacher wasn't in the classroom at 9 o'clock.

Unit 6

1 1 was ~~most~~ comfortable = more   2 The ~~better~~ day = best
3 a better bicycle ~~then~~ = than   4 the ~~beautifullest~~ car =
most beautiful   5 It's ~~much more hot~~ = much hotter
6 the ~~more~~ interesting place = most   7 ~~more cheapest~~ =
cheaper   8 ~~noisy and dirty~~ = noisier and dirtier

2 2 more expensive   3 the largest   4 nearer
5 the largest   6 better   7 the busiest

Unit 7

1 1 You ~~musn't~~ forget = mustn't.   2 You must ~~have to~~ bring =
must bring   3 They should ~~to~~ visit = should visit
4 You should ~~came~~ = come   5 Students ~~must'nt~~ use =
mustn't   6 You ~~don't~~ be late! = mustn't   7 We must ~~to~~
bring = must bring   8 You ~~shall~~ be here at four o'clock =
should

2 1 slowly   2 carefully   3 terribly   4 well   5 fast
6 easily   7 early   8 magically   9 quietly
10 wonderfully   11 comfortably   12 happily

Unit 8

1 1 Everyone ~~are~~ doing = was   2 it was ~~rainning~~ = raining
3 It ~~rained~~ a lot = was raining   4 I ~~will look~~ = was looking
5 We ~~was~~ playing = were   6 The kids ~~are~~ playing = were
7 I ~~watched~~ = was watching   8 you ~~was~~ working = were

2 1 were sleeping, was cleaning (or cleaned)   2 bought,
was visiting   3 were swimming, saw   4 were watching,
phoned   5 was studying, heard   6 saw, was shopping

Unit 9

1 **1** My mother ~~going~~ = ' s (is) going   **2** I ~~go~~ visit = 'm (am) going to   **3** We ~~gone~~ to play = 're (are) going   **4** ~~Im~~ going = I'm   **5** We are ~~goig~~ = going   **6** My friends are not ~~goin~~ to go = going   **7** My mum ~~gonna~~ buy = 's (is) going to   **8** I ~~went~~ travel = 'm (am) going to

2 **1** meeting   **2** doing   **3** playing   **4** to tidy   **5** to buy   **6** going

Unit 10

1 **1** 'll (will) visit   **2** may drive   **3** may go   **4** won't (will not) have   **5** 'll (will) buy   **6** won't (will not) be

2 **1** 'll (will) go, snows   **2** is, 'll (will) swim   **3** won't (will not) get, don't (do not) follow   **4** don't (do not) close, will run   **5** 'll (will) fall, aren't (are not)   **6** are, 'll (will) go

Unit 11

1 **1** I ~~took~~ a lot of photos = 've (have) taken   **2** I ~~go~~ been = 've (have)   **3** It ~~was~~ been hot = 's (has)   **4** We ~~had~~ sun = 've (have) had   **5** I've just ~~wached~~ = watched   **6** I have ~~ritten~~ = written   **7** I've ~~choosed~~ = chosen

2 (Suggested answers)

2 How long have you known your best friend? (I've known him / her for six years.)

3 How long has your teacher worked in your school? (He / She's worked in my school since 2008.)

4 How long have you had your school bag? (I've had it since my birthday.)

5 How long has your school been open? (It's been open since 1989.)

6 How long have your parents lived here? (They've lived here for 15 years.)

Unit 12

1 **1** is called   **2** are downloaded   **3** were watched   **4** weren't (were not) given   **5** isn't (is not) made   **6** was repaired

2 **2** is spoken all over the world   **3** was phoned while I was in class   **4** was built in 1965   **5** isn't (is not) used very much   **6** wasn't (was not) taught at my school until four years ago

Workbook key & scripts

Unit 1

Grammar

1 **3** We've / have got six cousins.

4 Have you got any sisters?

5 She hasn't got any brothers.

6 Harry's / has got very short fair hair.

7 Has Molly got a nickname?

8 We haven't / have not got our trainers.

2 **2** I ~~get~~ – have got / 've got

3 it ~~had~~ got – has

4 ~~has got~~ – is

5 There ~~has got~~ lots of – are

6 The handbag ~~has got black colour~~. – is black

7 ~~I'm~~ a lot of exams – I've got / have got

8 ~~Have you got an age~~ between – Are you

3 **2** walks to school, doesn't walk to school   **3** has lunch
4 does, doesn't do   **5** watches   **6** goes to bed

4 **2** How   **3** What   **4** Where   **5** Who   **6** When

5 (Suggested answers)

2 He drives to work. / He goes to work on the bus. / He goes to work by train.

3 I have toast and cereal. / I have cheese and ham.

4 My school is near my house.

5 My best friend is Susan.

6 They come to my house every evening.

Vocabulary

1 & 2

2 daughter   **3** uncle   **4** cousins   **5** husband
6 grandparents   **7** grandmother

---

 1 Recording script

1 I've got one brother but I haven't got any sisters.
2 I am my parents' only daughter.
3 My aunt Diana is married to my uncle Jacob.
4 Diana and Jacob have got two sons, Ben and Joe. Ben and Joe are my favourite cousins.
5 My aunt Katie hasn't got a husband – she doesn't want to get married yet.
6 My grandparents (my mum's mother and father) are both 65 years old.
7 My grandfather is one month younger than my grandmother.

---

3 & 4

2 f   **3** d   **4** e   **5** b   **6** g   **7** a

---

2 Recording script

1 Daisy has got a pair of trainers to wear for a basketball lesson.
2 Freddie has got some pencils for drawing pictures.
3 Daisy has got a diary to write homework in.
4 Freddie has got a mobile to call mum at lunchtime.
5 Daisy has got some money in a blue purse.
6 Freddie has got a snack because teenagers are always hungry!
7 Daisy has got a towel for a swimming lesson.

---

5 Freddie's bag: b, d, f

Daisy's bag: a, c, g, i

Exam tasks

Reading Part 2

1 C   **2** B   **3** C   **4** A   **5** B

Writing Part 6

1 trainers   **2** twins   **3** violin   **4** dinner   **5** eyes

Listening Part 3

1 B   **2** A   **3** C   **4** B   **5** A

---

3 Recording script

Listen to Kelly talking to her mum about her violin lessons.

For each question, choose the right answer (A, B or C).

Woman: Kelly, I've just spoken to your violin teacher. You haven't got a lesson this week.

Girl: Is she ill, Mum?

Woman: No, she's on a course because she's doing an exam next month.

Girl: So when's my next lesson?

Woman: It'll be the 15th – you're missing this week, the 8th August and on the 22nd, your teacher's away again.

Girl: Right.

Woman: She said you need a new music book, too.

Girl: Oh, OK. Where can we get that?

Woman: Well, they haven't got any music at the library, I've looked before. The bookshop's cheaper than the music shop, so we'll get it there.

Girl: OK. Which day?

Woman: How about Thursday? Not tomorrow, I work late on Tuesdays and you've got dance club on Wednesday.

Girl: Fine. Will you pick me up after school?

Woman: No, I'll only finish work at quarter to four, so go home first. I'll pick you up there at 4 o'clock. Then we'll get to the shop about quarter past four.

Girl:	Right. Can we have our dinner in a café afterwards?
Woman:	OK. You know the burger restaurant's closed, but we can go and have a pizza. The fish cafe's too far from the shops.
Girl:	Great!

Unit 2

Grammar

1 2 Danny has band practice every day except Sunday.

3 Danny often goes to school in his dad's car.

4 Danny visits his grandfather on Sundays.

5 Danny has swimming club twice a week.

6 Danny never goes to stamp club.

2 2 I ~~every day played table tennis~~. – I played table tennis every day.

3 ~~was beautiful always~~ there – was always beautiful

4 ~~Always I watch~~ the competition – I always watch

5 I ~~can usually once a week write~~. – I can usually write once a week.

6 The weather ~~sometimes was good~~ – The weather was sometimes good / Sometimes the weather was good

3 & 4
2 do you like **3** 'd / would like **4** Would you like
5 'd / would like **6** Do you like **7** like **8** 'd / would like

---

◉ 4 Recording script

Julian:	Did you go to Music Club yesterday?
Peter:	No, they played jazz and I don't like jazz much.
Julian:	What kind of music do you like?
Peter:	Rock, pop, classical ... most kinds, but not jazz!
Julian:	I'd like to come too. Can I just come or do I have to ask the teacher first?
Peter:	Just come when you want to. Would you like to come with me next week?
Julian:	Yes, please. I'd like to join so I can learn to play an instrument.
Peter:	Do you like all kinds of music?
Julian:	I like modern music best, but I'd like to learn more about classical and jazz, too.
Peter:	Music Club will be perfect for you!

Vocabulary

1 2 camping **3** tennis **4** camera **5** music **6** stamp **7** art

2 a Celia **b** Terry **c** Sarah **d** Harry **e** Natalia **f** Greg
g Jack

---

3 & 4
2 loves **3** doesn't like **4** enjoy **5** terrible at **6** prefers
7 interested in

◉ 5 Recording script

1 Ellie loves watching films. Maisie hates watching films.
2 Ellie hates cooking. Maisie loves cooking.
3 Ellie enjoys singing. Maisie doesn't like singing.
4 Ellie likes going to concerts. Maisie doesn't enjoy going to concerts.
5 Ellie is very good at playing computer games. Maisie is terrible at playing computer games.
6 Ellie likes dancing more than doing sports. Maisie prefers doing sports to dancing.
7 Ellie thinks history is boring. Maisie is interested in history.

---

5 (Suggested answers)

1 I love / hate / don't like cooking.

2 I love / hate / don't like singing.

3 I'm (not) good / bad / terrible at dancing.

4 I'm (not) interested in science.

5 I (don't) enjoy / like / hate / love / 'm good at / 'm bad at playing computer games.

6 I (don't) enjoy / like / hate / love going to the cinema.

Exam tasks

Reading Part 3a

1 B **2** C **3** C **4** B **5** A

Listening Part 4

1 2 Saturdays **3** Caponacre **4** Camilla **5** 6.45 pm **6** $3.50

◉ 6 Recording script

One

Teenage girl:	Which day does Stamp Club meet this week?
Teenage boy:	On Thursday.

Two

Teenage boy:	When do you usually go shopping?
Teenage girl:	On Saturdays.

Three

Teenage girl:	How do you spell your surname?
Teenage boy:	C-A-P-O-N-A-C-R-E.

Four

Teenage boy:	How do you spell your first name?
Teenage girl:	C-A-M-I-double L-A.

Five

Teenage girl:	What time does the bus leave this evening?
Teenage boy:	Quarter to seven.

Six

Teenage boy: How much is the book?
Teenage girl: Three dollars fifty.

2 **1** 20 / twenty   **2** bread   **3** Donagh   **4** 3.45   **5** 3.75

🔊 7 Recording script

You will hear a girl, Becky, telling her friend, Milo, about a cookery club.

Listen and complete each question.

Becky	Milo, did you know Cookery Club's starting again?
Milo	Really? Is it on Wednesday, like last year?
Becky	No, Friday. Mr Bath told me to tell everyone.
Milo	OK. Are many people doing it this year?
Becky	The new cookery room's got 12 cookers, so Mr Bath says 20 people can join.
Milo	Did he say what we're going to cook this week?
Becky	He's teaching us to make bread. And he'll bring some soup for us to have with it.
Milo	Great!
Becky	Mr Bath won't be here next week, so Miss Donagh will show us how to make something.
Milo	Who? How do you spell her name?
Becky	She's my science teacher. It's D-O-N-A-G-H.
Milo	OK. So is it the same time as last year?
Becky	Yes. School finishes at 3.30, and we all need time to get to the cookery room, so we'll meet at three forty-five, like last year.
Milo	Right. And how much is it?
Becky	It'll be different every week, but not more than £4.50. This week it's £3.75.
Milo	OK. See you there!

Writing Part 7

1 to   **2** at   **3** have   **4** and   **5** Do   **6** of   **7** is   **8** take
9 Would   **10** than

Unit 3

Grammar

1 **2** Are, any   **3** is, some   **4** is, a   **5** isn't, a
6 isn't, any   **7** are, any

2 **2** How much milk is there in the fridge?

   3 How many flowers are there in the garden?

   4 How many pictures are there in the hall?

   5 How much meat is there on the plate?

   6 How many potatoes are there in the bag?

   7 How much jam is there on the bread?

3 & 4

   2 There's a little milk in the fridge.

   3 There are a lot of flowers in the garden.

   4 There are a few pictures in the hall.

   5 There's a little meat on the plate.

   6 There are a lot of potatoes in the bag.

   7 There's a little jam on the bread.

🔊 8 Recording script

1 How many apples are there in the bowl?
   There are a few apples in the bowl.

2 How much milk is there in the fridge?
   There's a little milk in the fridge.

3 How many flowers are there in the garden?
   There are a lot of flowers in the garden.

4 How many pictures are there in the hall?
   There are a few pictures in the hall.

5 How much meat is there on the plate?
   There's a little meat on the plate.

6 How many potatoes are there in the bag?
   There are a lot of potatoes in the bag.

7 How much jam is there on the bread?
   There's a little jam on the bread.

5 **3** has to tidy   **4** doesn't have to tidy   **5** have to tidy
   6 has to wash   **7** have to make   **8** doesn't have to wash
   9 doesn't have to clean   **10** has to clean

Vocabulary

1

S	O	F	A	C	H	L	O	P
F	D	O	C	O	L	F	M	B
C	U	P	B	O	A	R	D	E
H	W	A	E	K	M	I	E	M
A	D	E	A	E	P	D	S	O
I	C	H	M	R	M	G	K	F
R	S	S	H	O	W	E	R	A
T	T	O	I	L	E	T	J	U
H	O	F	M	I	R	R	O	R

a cupboard   **b** chair   **c** lamp   **d** toilet   **e** shower
f fridge   **g** cooker   **h** sofa   **i** desk   **j** mirror

2 **2** bathroom   **3** living room   **4** bedroom   **5** kitchen   **6** hall

3 & 4

   2 ~~red or blue~~ white or brown

   3 ~~fruit~~ vegetables / fish

   4 ~~eat~~ drink

   5 ~~hot~~ cold

   6 ~~plant~~ bird

   7 ~~trees or flowers~~ the sea or rivers / lakes

   8 ~~square~~ round

🔊 9 Recording script

1 An omelette is made from eggs.
2 Rice is usually white or brown.

3 People usually make soup with meat or vegetables (or fish).

4 Juice is nice to drink.

5 Salad is usually cold.

6 Chickens are a kind of bird.

7 Fish live in the sea or rivers (and lakes).

8 Onions are round.

Exam tasks

Reading part 5

1 B   2 B   3 C   4 C   5 A   6 C   7 A   8 A

Listening Part 5

1 vegetables   2 school(s)   3 0996 548013   4 Monday(s)
5 5.15 / quarter past five / 5

⊙10 Recording script

You will hear a woman on the TV talking about a new programme for teenagers. Listen and complete each question.

Woman: Sadly, that was the last *Cook it Fast* show, but don't worry, food lovers! There will soon be an exciting new show for teenagers called *Hot Food*. The show will include cooking and information about all kinds of subjects such as healthy food and national dishes. In the first programme, young cooks tell us all about vegetables. They'll show us how to cook and grow them. But this won't be like a normal cookery show: the programmes are not filmed at the TV centre. We're making the programmes in schools! And we'd like you to call us with your ideas – we'll choose the best ones and then come and film you! So phone us on 0996 548013 if you have any brilliant ideas for the programmes. Now get out your diary! This amazing new programme will be on Mondays. And on Tuesday evenings, you'll be able to chat to people from the show online. The first show's on 28th November, after you come home from school, from five fifteen until five forty-five – write it down now!

Writing Part 8

1 10.30 / ten thirty   2 raincoat   3 coach   4 make cheese
5 8.50

Unit 4

Grammar

1 2 are you going   3 aren't / are not / 're not going
4 are / 're going   5 is / 's moving   6 are you doing
7 am / 'm waiting   8 am / 'm going

2 2 He's / is fishing.

3 He isn't drinking (anything).

4 He's / is wearing a cap, jeans and a T-shirt.

5 He's / is sitting (on a box/by the sea).

6 He's / is eating (some chips).

7 He isn't reading.

3 2 practise   3 is, doing   4 doesn't want   5 'm / am playing
6 play   7 'm / am not doing   8 does, have   9 'm / am writing

Vocabulary

1 2 swimming   3 basketball   4 snowboarding
5 volleyball   6 cycling   7 ice-skating   8 surfing
9 skateboarding   10 football

2 2 h   3 a   4 b   5 i   6 e   7 j   8 c   9 g   10 d

3 2 golf   3 hockey   4 table tennis   5 athletics
6 martial arts   7 aerobics

4 2 g   3 c   4 f   5 a   6 d   7 e

5 & 6
2 go   3 do   4 throw   5 train   6 lose

⊙11 Recording script

1 Do you play volleyball in a team?

2 I'd like to go cycling when we're on holiday.

3 Janey and Maria do aerobics every Monday evening.

4 You must throw the ball over the net.

5 How often do you train for the competition with your coach?

6 I won't be happy if we lose the match.

---

7 skirt c   trousers c   jacket b   trainers d
jeans c   boots d   shorts c   coat b   hat a
shirt b   sweater b   dress b and c

Exam tasks

Listening Part 1

1 A   2 C   3 B   4 B   5 C

Listening Part 1, Exam task

⊙12 Recording script

You will hear five short conversations.

There is one question for each conversation.

For each question, choose the right answer (A, B or C).

1   *Where is Jessie playing table tennis?*
Girl: Where's your sister, Robert?
Boy: Jessie's playing table tennis with her friend, Kate. They went after school.
Girl: To Kate's house, you mean?
Boy: That's right, and they're going to the sports centre to play volleyball after that.

2   *What does the girl's football team wear?*
Boy: Does your team wear black shirts, like ours?
Girl: With white numbers, yes. Our team wears nearly the same as yours, but our socks are white, not black.
Boy: Oh. So you wear white shorts, too?
Girl: We do, with a black number at the sides.

---

3   What time is Henry's skiing lesson?

Man: Is your skiing lesson before or after mine, Henry?

Boy: What time's yours, Dad?

Man: 8.45.

Boy: Oh, well mine starts half an hour later, at quarter past nine. You'll have to get up before me!

4   What is Mum's aerobics teacher doing this evening?

Boy: Why aren't you at your aerobics class this evening, Mum?

Woman: Our teacher can't do the class this week.

Boy: Is she ill again?

Woman: No, she's fine now. She's flying to Paris tonight because she's got a wedding there tomorrow.

5   Where did Liz sell her football ticket?

Boy: Liz, hi. Did you sell that football match ticket that you don't want? I just heard someone on the radio asking for tickets.

Girl: Oh, I've sold mine. I put a poster up at my football club and someone there wanted it.

Boy: That's good.

Girl: Yes, Dad advertised it online first, but no one called us about that.

Reading Part 4

1 B **2** B **3** A **4** B **5** C **6** B **7** A

Writing Part 9

(Suggested answer)

Hi Ali

My nearest sports centre is in my village, next to the park. You can play badminton, squash and volleyball there and it's got a swimming pool. I never go because I don't like sports!

Bye,

Unit 5

Grammar

1 **2** drank **3** ate **4** enjoyed **5** tried **6** found **7** opened

2 & 3

2 was **3** started **4** didn't stop **5** didn't do **6** didn't sleep **7** were **8** invited **9** had **10** didn't mind **11** played **12** didn't hear

---

⊙ 13 Recording script

Last summer, Simon went with his family to camp in a tent near a castle in the mountains. It was a beautiful place but as soon as they arrived it started to rain and it didn't stop for four days! During the day, they didn't do any activities because it was too wet outside and at night, they didn't sleep because the wind and the rain were so noisy. On the fifth day, the man who lived in the castle invited them to stay inside the castle! After that, Simon and his family had a great time. They didn't mind the bad weather because they played games in the castle all day and they didn't hear the rain and the wind at night.

---

4 **2** When were you born? I was born on ....

3 What time did you get up this morning? I got up at ....

4 Where did you go last weekend? I went to ....

5 What did you have for breakfast today? I had ....

5 **1** ago **2** at **3** on **4** in **5** on **6** in

Vocabulary

1 **2** b **3** c **4** a **5** f **6** e

2 **1** d **2** e **3** c **4** f **5** b **6** a

3 **2** supermarket **3** newsagent **4** department store **5** bank **6** bookshop

4 **2** 3/8/1492   Christopher Columbus set sail from Spain

3 10/3/1876   the first telephone call

4 4/7/1776   American independence from Britain

5 17/12/1903   the first aeroplane flight

6 20/7/1969   the first step on the moon

Exam tasks

Reading Part 2

1 A **2** C **3** A **4** B **5** C

Listening Part 5

1 **1** cinema **2** 25th November **3** clothes **4** boat **5** 5.75

2 **1** What's the address of the museum? It's in Victoria Square.

2 What's the name of the exhibition? It's called Cinema.

3 When does / will the exhibition end? It ends on 25th November.

4 What is in the new fashion room? There are clothes worn by famous pop stars.

5 Are there any cheap travel tickets? Yes – boat tickets

6 How much does it cost for teenagers? £5.75

⊙ 14 Recording script

You will hear some information about a museum.

Listen and complete each question.

The Museum of Pop Music is the city's most popular museum for visitors aged 12 to 18. And its new address in Victoria Square has brought thousands more visitors to see its amazing collections.

This month, the museum has a new exhibition. It's called 'Cinema' and it explores art and music from film, with hundreds of pictures, recordings and videos. It's open from the 31st October until the 25th November. Don't miss it! The museum has also just opened a new fashion room. Here, you can see a large number of clothes worn by famous pop stars over the last fifty or sixty years.

To make it easier for you to travel to the museum, why don't you come on the boat? Museum visitors can now buy special low-price tickets. It's much nicer than sitting on a bus! Ask about this at any transport office or online.

Museum tickets for adults cost eight pounds fifty, but for children it's just five pounds seventy-five. This includes young people up to the age of 19, but children under five go free.

Writing Part 9

(Suggested answer)

Dear Zoe

I went to town with Mum yesterday. I brought a great CD in the new shop in the shopping centre. We went home and we danced in the kitchen!

See you soon,

James

Unit 6

Grammar

1 **1** bigger **2** more expensive **3** slower
   4 smaller **5** busier **6** faster

2 **2** the most easy way = the easiest way

   3 the most cheapest way = the cheapest way

   4 your most old clothes = your oldest clothes

   5 the beast competitions = the best competitions

   6 the most big shopping centre = the biggest shopping centre

   7 the more interesting place = the most interesting place

   8 the bigest cities = the biggest cities

3 & 4

3 Journey B is further than journey C.

4 Journey A is the longest.

5 Journey B is cheaper than journey A.

6 Journey A is the most expensive.

7 Train B is older than train C.

8 Train C is the newest.

---

15 Recording script

1 Journey C is longer than journey A.
2 Journey A is the shortest.
3 Journey B is further than journey C.
4 Journey A is the longest.
5 Journey B is cheaper than journey A.
6 Journey A is the most expensive.
7 Train B is older than train C.
8 Train C is the newest.

Vocabulary

1 **2** B, C **3** A, C **4** E, F **5** B, C **6** B, C, F
   7 E, F **8** B, F **9** B, F **10** A, C

2 & 3

   2 walk **3** fly **4** drive **5** ride **6** sail

3 (girl's answers)
   1 train **2** car **3** Barcelona airport **4** No.
   5 My uncle **6** (I don't know.) About 3 months

---

16 Recording script

Narrator: One

Boy: How do you usually travel when you go on holiday?
Girl: We usually travel by train.

Narrator: Two

Boy: Do most students walk to your school or do they go by bus or car?
Girl: Most go by car!

Narrator: Three

Boy: Which airport do people in your town fly from?
Girl: They usually fly from Barcelona airport.

Narrator: Four

Boy: Can 10-year-olds drive cars in your country?
Girl: No, of course they can't!

Narrator: Five

Boy: Does anyone in your family ride a motorbike?
Girl: Yes. My uncle rides one.

Narrator: Six

Boy: How long does it take for a ship to sail around the world?
Girl: I don't know. How long?
Boy: About three months, I think.

---

4 **2** turn right **3** Festival Bridge **4** your left **5** turn left **6** in front of

5 (Suggested answer)

Walk to John Street and turn left. Walk down John Street until you get to Park Street. Turn left. Walk down Park Street, then turn right into Green Lane. Walk down to the river and go across Pool Bridge. The swimming pool is on your right.

Exam tasks

Reading Part 3b

1 E **2** G **3** C **4** D **5** A

Listening Part 2

1 Michael C **2** David B **3** Ellen E **4** Katy A **5** Tom F

---

17 Recording script

Listen to Marcia talking to her friend, Josh, about taking the school bus.

Where does each person catch the school bus?

Write a letter A–H next to each person.

Marcia: I'm going to start taking the school bus next week, Josh. Where should I catch it?

Josh:	I catch it from Hill Street. After the railway bridge, there's a roundabout and my bus stop's there.
Marcia:	Right. Does Michael catch it there? He lives near you.
Josh:	No. His mum drives him into town. She works at the motorbike shop, but leaves her car in the car park in George Street. Michael catches the bus there.
Marcia:	Right.
Josh:	David gets on at the bus stop in New Street, by the bridge – the one that crosses the river.
Marcia:	Oh yes, I can catch it there, too. Who else goes on the bus?
Josh:	Ellen. She lives opposite the cinema, so she catches the bus at the tram stop near there.
Marcia:	What about Katy, Ellen's neighbour?
Josh:	She doesn't like crossing the busy road to the tram stop. So she uses the stop next to the traffic lights behind the station.
Marcia:	Oh yes.
Josh:	Tom gets the bus too, at the crossing, near the supermarket car park.
Marcia:	I know. Thanks Josh ...

Writing Part 7

1 at **2** have **3** on **4** than **5** the **6** by **7** takes **8** would
9 so **10** this

Unit 7

Grammar

1 **2** mustn't listen **3** mustn't chew **4** must take
5 mustn't use **6** mustn't eat **7** mustn't talk
8 must show **9** mustn't ride **10** must put

2 (Suggested answers)
You mustn't talk. You mustn't eat. You must be quiet.
You must turn your mobile off.

3 & 4
2 a **3** c **4** f **5** e **6** b

---

18 Recording script

Girl:	Peter is always hungry in the afternoon at school.
Boy:	He should eat more at lunchtime.
Girl:	Peter often forgets what his homework is.
Boy:	He should write it down in a diary or notebook.
Girl:	On rainy days, Peter's sweater is always wet.
Boy:	He should wear a jacket.
Girl:	Peter wants to play tennis better.
Boy:	He should take some lessons.
Girl:	Peter is always tired in the morning.
Boy:	He shouldn't go to bed late.
Girl:	Peter's sister is angry with him.
Boy:	He shouldn't borrow her things without asking.

---

5 (Suggested answers)
2 Paul wants to be healthier. He shouldn't eat chocolate.
3 Franz wants to learn about sea animals. He should look on the Internet.
4 Suzannah wants to make some new friends. She should join a club.
5 Anita wants to grow her hair long. She shouldn't go to the hairdresser's.
6 Henry doesn't like the colour of his bedroom walls. He should paint them a different colour.

6 **4** Aysha can speak English now.
5 Aysha couldn't speak English in 2007.
6 Aysha couldn't surf in 2010.
7 Aysha could surf in 2012.
8 Aysha could swim in 2008.
9 Aysha can ski now.
10 Aysha couldn't ski in 2009.
11 Aysha couldn't play the keyboard in 2008.

7 **2** you ~~could~~ come = you can come
3 you ~~can't~~ come to my party = you couldn't come to my party
4 to see if I ~~can~~ find = to see if I could find
5 I ~~can't~~ believe it = I couldn't believe it
6 you couldn't ~~came~~ = you couldn't come
7 so you ~~will~~ come on foot = so you can come on foot
8 we ~~coughtn't~~ go = we couldn't go
9 we can ~~doing~~ the homework = we can do the homework

8 **2** quickly **3** terrible **4** slowly **5** quietly **6** comfortable
7 happily

Vocabulary

1 **1** music **2** maths **3** science **4** history **5** geography
6 art **7** English

2 & 3
1 has **2** studies **3** teaches **4** spends **5** missed

---

19 Recording script

One
Boy: Hassan only has lessons at school in the morning.

Two
Boy: Hassan studies fourteen different subjects at school.

Three
Boy: A man called Mr Ali teaches Hassan maths.

Four
Boy: Hassan spends about two hours a night doing his homework.

Five
Boy: Hassan has only missed one day of school this school year.

---

4 2 guitar c   3 violin a   4 keyboard b   5 piano e

Exam tasks

Reading Part 1

1 B   2 H   3 A   4 G   5 F

Listening Part 5

1 guitar   2 Wednesday(s)   3 58   4 Play Well   5 22.80

---

 20 Recording script

Narrator: You will hear a music teacher talking about her lessons.

Listen and complete each question.

I'm here to tell you about my after-school music lessons at Hill Road School. I'm Mrs Sweet. I know some of you can already play the violin because you learn it in music lessons at school, and I've seen you playing in the school orchestra. But if you'd like to try something else, you can learn to play the guitar with me. I have a class of ten students and we have lots of fun! School orchestra practises on Mondays, and I think it's good for you to have a rest on Tuesdays, so you can come and play more music at my lessons on Wednesdays, starting at four o'clock. We meet for the lessons in Room fifty-eight – that's the big room opposite Art Room seven. If you come, you must buy the book I use so you can practise at home. It's called *Play Well* and you can buy it at Music Now. My lessons aren't expensive because you learn in a group of ten. Each student pays just £22.80 a month, so it's five pounds seventy a week. OK?

Writing Part 9

1 1 opening and closing formulae

2 Me, I like French music: Eddy Mitchell and Johnny Hallyday are my <u>favourite</u> French singers. I <u>also</u> <u>like</u> English music. The Beatles is the <u>best</u> group that I have ever <u>heard</u>. If you want, I can play the bass in the concert. I <u>am</u> going to <u>have</u> a meeting about the concert. Phone me on 3466 for more information <u>about</u> this. Thank you.

2 (Suggested answer)

Hi Nicky,

In our music lessons, we sometimes sing and we sometimes play the keyboard. I like rock music best but I also like some folk music. I'd love to learn to play the drums.

Bye,

Unit 8

Grammar

1 2 He was sleeping.

3 They were singing.

4 They were talking / chatting / having / drinking coffee.

5 They were laughing.

6 She was studying.

7 student's own answer

2 2 He wasn't dancing.

3 They weren't studying.

4 They weren't singing.

5 They weren't drinking coffee.

6 She wasn't laughing.

7 I wasn't doing an exam.

3 & 4

1 didn't stop, was watching   2 dropped, was putting   3 saw, were walking   4 broke, was trying   5 was playing, didn't hear   6 built, were camping

---

 21 Recording script

1 He didn't stop laughing while he was watching the cartoon.

2 She dropped the bowl on her foot while she was putting fruit in it.

3 They saw the circus lorries in the street while they were walking to school.

4 He broke the light on his bike while he was trying to mend the wheel.

5 She was playing a computer game so she didn't hear the phone.

6 We built a fire for the first time while we were camping.

Vocabulary

1 2 campsite   3 capital   4 adventure   5 hotel   6 guidebook   7 island

2 2 a   3 b   4 a   5 a   6 b

3 2 terrible   bad   OK

3 not bad   good   amazing

4 boring   all right   interesting

5 OK   good   brilliant

6 boring   good   exciting

Exam tasks

Listening Part 2

1 C   2 H   3 A   4 G   5 E

---

 22 Recording script

Listen to Matthew talking to his friend, Alice, about courses his friends took while they were on holiday.

Which course did each friend take?

For questions 1–5, write a letter A–H next to each friend.

Matthew: How was your holiday, Alice?

Alice: Great. My course was really interesting.

Matthew: What did you learn?

Alice: How to write stories and news articles.

Matthew: Really? Maybe I should do a course on my holiday ...

Alice: Like Ahmet? He learned to cook Chinese dishes on holiday – he wants to work as a food writer when he leaves school.

Matthew:	Zena went to the same holiday camp as Ahmet, didn't she?
Alice:	Yes, but she chose a course which she didn't need to do lots of reading and writing for. She had a week of Spanish dancing lessons.
Matthew:	What about Zena's sister, Leah?
Alice:	She learned to work with silver and made a beautiful necklace and earrings. I saw them yesterday.
Matthew:	That's amazing. Is Mick on holiday?
Alice:	No, he just went away for two days because he had to come home on Monday to do a music exam. He did a windsurfing and sailing course at Lake Jarvis.
Matthew:	Right. When does Ellie come home?
Alice:	Next week. She's done a short course on biology this week. It was all about water plants and she loved it.
Matthew:	Really?

Reading Part 4

1 B **2** B **3** B **4** A **5** C **6** B **7** A

Writing Part 8

1 taxi **2** Pizza Palace **3** High Town **4** 65 **5** bridges.com

Unit 9

Grammar

1 & 2

2 f **3** d **4** e **5** a **6** b

> **23 Recording script**
>
> 1 He's carrying his violin because he's going to play in a concert.
> 2 He's revising because he's going to do an exam tomorrow.
> 3 He's waiting in the street because a bus is going to come soon.
> 4 He's finding his seat in the theatre because the play is going to start soon
> 5 He's practising dancing because he's going to a disco later.
> 6 He needs a knife because he's going to cut the bread.

3 **2** Are you going to get up early tomorrow?

3 Is it going to rain?

4 Is he going to go to Portugal?

5 Are you going to go to basketball practice?

6 Is it going to stop soon?

7 Are we going to have dinner soon?

4 **2** to take **3** speaking **4** to find **5** writing **6** practising **7** sitting

Vocabulary

1 **2** play **3** concert **4** circus **5** disco / dance **6** exhibition

2 **1** b **2** d **3** a **4** e **5** c

3 **2** a writer **3** a musician **4** an artist **5** a musician **6** an actor **7** a singer **8** an artist

Exam tasks

Reading Part 3b

1 A **2** E **3** F **4** B **5** G

Listening Part 4

1 photos / photographs **2** 24th / 24 **3** college **4** 30 **5** colour

> **24 Recording script**
>
> *You will hear Neil talking to his friend about an art exhibition.*
>
> *Listen and complete each question.*
>
> | | |
> |---|---|
> | Neil: | Maria, do you like this painting? |
> | Maria: | It's brilliant, Neil! Did you do it? |
> | Neil: | Yes. I'm going to put it in the art club's Young Artists' exhibition. |
> | Maria: | Great. Will the exhibition only be paintings? Or other things as well, like drawings or film? |
> | Neil: | There are going to be a few photos in the exhibition too. |
> | Maria: | Really? I must see it. When is it? |
> | Neil: | In July, starting on the 24th and finishing on the 30th. Can you come? |
> | Maria: | Yes. Where is it? |
> | Neil: | At the college. The exhibition entrance is opposite the theatre. |
> | Maria: | OK. Are you going to sell the paintings? |
> | Neil: | Yes, but quite cheaply. We decided the most expensive price should be £30, but some of the small pictures will cost just £7.50. And we'll give all the money we get to our art club. |
> | Maria: | That's good. |
> | Neil: | And our teacher is going to give lessons at the exhibition. |
> | Maria: | What about? |
> | Neil: | She's a really good painter of people. But the subject she's going to teach at the exhibition is colour – so all sorts of artists will be interested. |

Writing

1 **1** but **2** and **3** or **4** because

2 (Suggested answer)

Hi Paddy,

I'm sorry, I can't come to the cinema with you on Wednesday because I'm going to visit my grandma. Can we go on Friday instead? I'd like to see 'Snow Flight'.

Harry

Unit 10

Grammar

1 **2** may   **3** won't   **4** may   **5** will   **6** won't

2 & 3

  2 goes, 'll need   **3** takes, won't need   **4** cycles, 'll feel
  5 sees, 'll take   **6** 'll put, starts   **7** won't take, is

> **●25 Recording script**
>
> 1 She'll go to the lake with Nick if he doesn't have football practice.
> 2 If she goes to the lake, she'll need her swimming costume.
> 3 If she takes a picnic, she won't need to buy food in the café.
> 4 If she cycles around the lake, she'll feel tired.
> 5 If she sees some interesting animals, she'll take photos of them.
> 6 She'll put her camera in her bag if it starts to rain.
> 7 She won't take her rain jacket if the weather is good.

4 **2** I ~~am~~ fat = I'll be fat   **3** If you like we ~~would~~ go = If you like, we'll go   **4** If I can I ~~am going~~. = If I can, I'll go.
5 when ~~you'll arrive~~ = when you arrive   **6** you ~~would not~~ find it here = you won't find it here

Vocabulary

1 **2** on a river   **3** in a field   **4** on a path   **5** by a gate
  6 on a hill   **7** in a wood   **8** on a lake

2 **2** summer   **3** winter   **4** autumn   **5** winter   **6** spring
  7 autumn

3 **a** ice   **b** wind   **c** storm   **d** fog   **e** cloud   **f** thunderstorm
  g sun   **h** snow   **i** rain

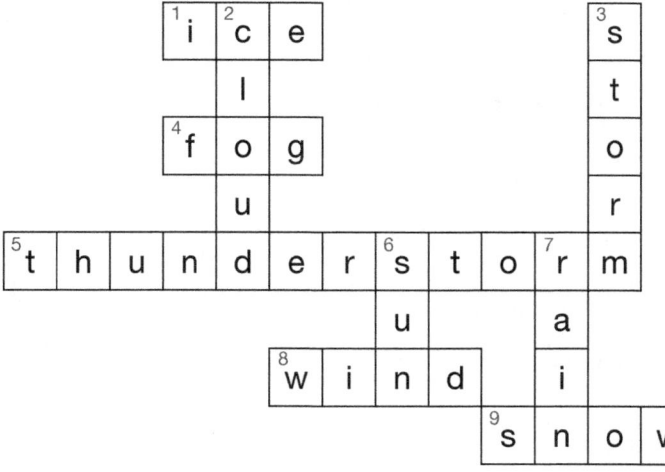

Exam tasks

Listening Part 1

1 B   **2** A   **3** C   **4** A   **5** B

Writing Part 8

1 9.15   **2** Mike Moon   **3** boots   **4** free   **5** station

---

> **●26 Recording script**
>
> *You will hear five short conversations.*
>
> *There is one question for each conversation.*
>
> *For each question, choose the right answer (A, B or C).*
>
> *1*   *What was the weather like last winter?*
> Man: Look at the snow outside, Daisy!
> Daisy: Wow! We can go skiing this weekend, brilliant! We didn't ski last winter at all, did we?
> Man: No, it was too wet. But there may be a lot of ice on the roads this weekend, so we may not go skiing.
> Daisy: Never mind.
>
> *2*   *Who will go for the birthday meal with Jade and her parents?*
> Woman: Who's coming to the restaurant with us on your birthday, Jade?
> Girl: I asked three of my best friends, Mary, Kate and Emma, but Emma can't come.
> Woman: OK, and of course your brother will be with us.
> Girl: And you and dad.
>
> *3*   *What happened during the storm last week?*
> Boy: That storm was terrible last week, wasn't it?
> Girl: Yes! A tree fell across the river and the water came up onto the road near our school.
> Boy: Was the school OK?
> Girl: Yes, but we had to walk there every morning until the water went away.
>
> *4*   *What work does Eleanor do on the farm at weekends?*
> Boy: Which farm do you work on at weekends, Eleanor?
> Girl: The one next to the horse-riding school.
> Boy: Cool! They have thousands of chickens – do you have to collect their eggs?
> Girl: I do, and my friend Sue sells them in the farm shop.
>
> *5*   *Where is Richard's MP3 player?*
> Man: Why are you using my MP3 player, Richard?
> Richard: Because mine's in Mum's car and she's gone to see Grandma.
> Man: Are you sure? I saw it in the kitchen this morning.
> Richard: I know, but I went to the library after that. Mum drove me home, and she's just texted me to say she found it on one of the seats.

Reading Part 1

1 F   **2** G   **3** E   **4** A   **5** D

Unit 11

Grammar

1 **2** flown   **3** taken   **4** caught   **5** been   **6** seen   **7** been
  8 done   **9** heard   **10** eaten

2 & 3

2 yet **3** yet **4** already **5** just **6** yet

4 **2** have won **3** haven't eaten **4** has, drunk **5** have, sat **6** hasn't finished **7** have, read

5 **2** He's / He has been a waiter since 2012. He's / He has been a waiter for two years.

3 The cat hasn't eaten anything since Tuesday. The cat hasn't eaten anything for two days.

4 We've / We have lived in this house for eight years. We've / We have lived in this house since 2005.

5 I've / I have had this bike since I was twelve years old. I've / I have had this bike for five years.

6 She's / She has been in the shop for an hour. She's / She has been in the shop since three o'clock.

Vocabulary

1 **2** mouth **3** hand **4** teeth **5** arms **6** face **7** eyes **8** stomach **9** hair **10** back

2 **b** unhappy **c** glad **d** sorry **e** hungry **f** angry **g** sick **h** tired **i** thirsty

Exam tasks

Reading Part 5

1 C **2** C **3** A **4** B **5** A **6** C **7** B **8** C

Writing Part 6

1 unhappy **2** thirsty **3** glad **4** tired **5** hungry

Reading Part 3a

1 C **2** B **3** A **4** A **5** C

Listening Part 3

1 B **2** A **3** B **4** B **5** C

Unit 12

Grammar

1 **2** are put **3** is visited **4** is written **5** are shared **6** are seen **7** are spent

2 & 3

2 The first digital cameras were sold by a company called Logitech.

3 The first fridge was built by Jacob Perkins in 1834.

4 The first computer mouse was made of wood.

5 The first hairdryer was used by a French hairdresser.

6 The first text message was written on 3rd December 1992.

⊙29 Recording script

1 The first email was sent in 1971.

2 The first digital cameras were sold by a company called Logitech.

3 The first fridge was built by Jacob Perkins in 1834.

4 The first computer mouse was made of wood.

5 The first hairdryer was used by a French hairdresser.

6 The first text messages were written on the third of December 1992.

Vocabulary

1 a MP3 player **b** desktop computer (hard drive and screen) **c** laptop **d** digital camera **e** keyboard **f** mobile phone **g** email **h** mouse

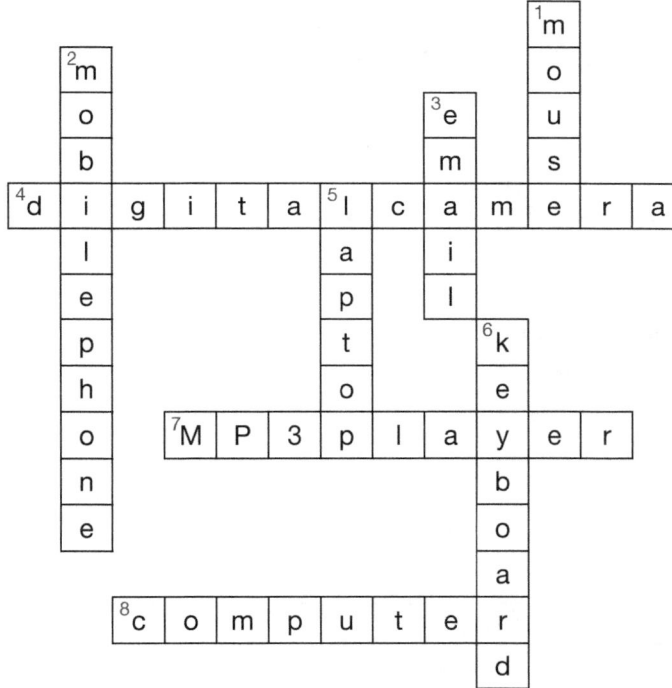

2 2 email address **3** screen **4** text **5** chat **6** laptop **7** click **8** internet

3 2 a **3** f **4** e **5** d **6** b

Exam tasks

Listening Part 2

1 A **2** G **3** E **4** B **5** H

⊙30 Recording script

Listen to Alice talking to her mum about finding things on the internet.

What thing does each person want to find?

For questions 1–5, write a letter A–H next to each person.

Woman: Hi, Alice.

Girl: Hi, Mum.

Woman: Where's everyone else? Is Aunt Sarah here?

Girl: She's on the computer with Dad. She's looking for a hairdryer that she saw on a TV advertisement.

Woman: What about your dad?

Girl: He wants a DVD. There's a special offer on that one about a photographer – he saw it at the cinema last year.

Woman: Oh, OK. And your brother?

Girl: Thomas is in his bedroom on his phone. He's trying to find a website where he can buy a cheap electric guitar. He wants to teach himself to play guitar.

Woman: Really? And your sister?

Girl: Annabelle's on her laptop. She's unhappy because our printer isn't good for photos, so she's looking for a new one.

Woman: Which cousin came with Aunt Sarah?

Girl: John. He's waiting to use the computer so he can look on the Internet. He wants this new digital camera that takes amazing pictures and videos.

Woman: Right. Is Grandma in her room?

Girl: Yes. She's online on her TV. She's asked for a new laptop for her birthday and she's looking at them now.

Woman: Right!

Reading Part 4

1 A **2** C **3** C **4** B **5** A **6** A **7** C

Writing Part 7

1 has **2** to **3** were/got **4** the **5** Of **6** but /though/ although **7** Why **8** with **9** be **10** does

Workbook vocabulary extra key

Unit 1

1 **1** Sara's grandmother **2** Sara's brother
3 Sara's father **4** Sara's mother

2 a grandfather **b** aunts **c** cousins **d** son
e daughter

2 **2** thirsty **3** fat **4** towel **5** terrible
6 yellow **7** pencil

Unit 2

1 **2** i **3** h **4** f **5** c **6** d **7** j **8** k **9** l **10** b
11 a **12** g

Pictures: 1, 5, 11, 12, 2, 3

Unit 3

1 **1** floor **2** sofa **3** bed **4** desk **5** table
6 chair **7** cupboard **8** lamp **9** cooker
10 ceiling **11** shelf **12** mirror

2

D	E	C	H	I	C	K	E	N	P
F	I	S	T	S	C	L	E	M	O
B	T	S	S	C	H	E	B	E	J
P	J	U	A	I	D	A	R	C	U
O	M	E	L	E	T	T	E	H	I
T	I	Y	A	X	S	A	A	E	C
A	M	L	D	W	O	F	D	E	E
T	U	O	P	W	U	I	Q	S	G
O	N	I	O	N	P	S	L	E	R
R	R	I	C	E	T	H	J	A	M

1 chicken **2** onion, potato **3** fish **4** soup
5 omelette **6** jam, juice **7** rice **8** cheese
9 bread **10** salad

Unit 4

1

2 **2** swimming costume **3** boots **4** trainers **5** trousers **6** scarf
7 jacket **8** dress **9** sweater **10** shoes **11** shorts **12** helmet
13 coat **14** jeans **15** socks **16** skirt

Unit 5

1 **1** f **2** h **3** a **4** b **5** e **6** d **7** g **8** i **9** c

2

1	1st	first
4	4th	fourth
9	9th	ninth
11	11th	eleventh
12	12th	twelfth
31	31st	thirty-first
25	25th	twenty-fifth
18	18th	eighteenth

Write	Say
May 12th	May the twelfth
27th January	the twenty-seventh of January
August 16th / 16th August	the sixteenth of August
February 23rd, 2001 / 23rd February, 2001	the twenty-third of February, two thousand and one
July 13th, 2008	July the thirteenth, two thousand and eight / the thirteenth of July, two thousand and eight
22nd December, 1994	December the twenty-second, nineteen ninety-four / the twenty-second of December, nineteen ninety-four
April 10th, 1887 / 10th April, 1887	April the tenth, eighteen eighty-seven

Unit 6

1 **1** Ships **2** coach **3** underground **4** helicopter **5** motorbike **6** Lorries

2 **1** car park **2** roundabout **3** bridge **4** park **5** traffic lights **6** crossing

Unit 7

1

history – reading about past events, learning about past kings and queens

music – playing an instrument, singing

science – studying how plants grow, learning about space

English – learning grammar rules, doing a listening test

geography – studying mountains and rivers, learning about weather in different countries

maths – learning about how to find the size of triangles, adding numbers

2 **1** keyboard **2** violin **3** piano **4** drum **5** guitar

Unit 8

1 **1** climbing **2** visiting **3** staying **4** having **5** speaking **6** trying

2 **2** amazing **3** tiring **4** terrible **5** interesting **6** brilliant

Unit 9

1 **1** an exhibition **2** a party **3** a disco **4** a concert **5** a circus **6** a film **7** a play

2 **1** F **2** T **3** F **4** T **5** F **6** F

Unit 10

1 **1** A **2** A & B **3** B **4** A & B **5** A & B **6** B **7** A **8** A

2

W	U	C	I	W	K	L	A	F	O	G	G
I	B	L	A	I	T	F	A	G	O	H	S
N	M	O	P	N	E	A	V	S	U	M	U
T	H	U	N	D	E	R	S	T	O	R	M
E	A	D	C	R	R	J	P	I	T	F	M
R	A	I	N	F	S	A	R	N	S	M	E
O	T	R	A	I	M	C	I	L	U	L	R
K	F	S	N	O	W	O	N	E	N	E	X
I	C	E	T	R	W	Q	G	M	J	O	P
A	S	Y	J	A	U	T	U	M	N	K	O

Unit 11

1 **1** F You see with your eyes. **2** T **3** T **4** T **5** F People have one nose. **6** T **7** F Your feet are at the end of your legs. **8** T **9** F You wear a hat on your head. **10** F People have two legs. **11** T **12** F You wear necklaces round your neck.

2 **1** c **2** d **3** f **4** a **5** b **6** e

Unit 12

1 **1** hairdryer – i **2** MP3 player – c **3** digital camera – d **4** mouse – f **5** keyboard – g **6** games console – b **7** laptop – e **8** mobile phone – a **9** printer – h **10** alarm clock – j

2

write	chat	play	text	watch	download	call	send	
				✓				TV
	✓	✓	✓		✓	✓		on a mobile phone
		✓			✓			a computer game
			✓	✓				a film from the Internet
✓			✓				✓	a message
✓							✓	an email
✓	✓							to friends online

Photocopiable resources

Unit 1

Recording script

Listen to Scott talking to his cousin Amanda about his school day.

For each question, choose the right answer (A, B or C).

Amanda: Hi, Scott! How are you?

Scott: Oh hi, Amanda! I'm tired!

Amanda: Well, don't go to bed so late!

Scott: But I don't. I watch sports on TV and then I go to bed at about nine fifteen. The problem is I wake up really early.

Amanda: Why's that?

Scott: I take the boat to school now, and it goes at half past seven in the morning, so my mum wakes us up at a quarter past six. We have breakfast and leave home at seven.

Amanda: So have you changed schools, then?

Scott: Yes. The school on our island is for six to eleven year olds. Now I'm twelve, I go to school on another island with my sister Tanya. She's fourteen now.

Amanda: Oh, I see. So do you get home late in the evening?

Scott: Quite late. The boat back home is two hours after school. My mum's sister lives near the school so we go and have dinner at her house.

Amanda: When do you have time to do your homework?

Scott: We usually find a quiet table on the boat. When we get home, we watch TV, listen to music or use the computer.

Amanda: And what's your new school like?

Scott: Great! I like my maths teacher best but the English and sports classes are cool, too!

Amanda: Sounds good! When can I come and visit?

Unit 2

Recording script

You will hear a boy, Ben, asking a friend about a cinema club.

Listen and complete each question.

Ben: Hello, Hannah.

Hannah: Hi, Ben.

Ben: Hannah, I'm thinking of joining the Cinema Club. You're a member, aren't you?

Hannah: Yes, I am. It's brilliant!

Ben: When do you meet?

Hannah: We meet once a week, on Monday afternoons.

Ben: What time?

Hannah: Well, some of us have got hockey training from 4 to 5 p.m. so the club meets at 5.15 p.m., when everyone can come.

Ben: That sounds OK. Do you still meet in the library?

Hannah: We've just moved to the computer room, which is opposite the library. It's got a much better screen.

Ben: Oh, yes. I know where it is. What do you do in the club?

Hannah: Well, one of us usually chooses a film, we watch it and then we talk about it. Last week, we saw *Push* with Dakota Fanning. Next week, we're going to watch *New Moon*. You know, the one with Taylor Lautner in it. You should come!

Ben: How much does it cost?

Hannah: It's £1.60 a week or £3.80 a month.

Ben: Cool! Who do I need to speak to?

Hannah: Send an email to jaykes at cinemaclub dot com . That's J–A–Y–K–E–S.

Ben: Great! I'll do that tonight.

Unit 4

Recording script

You will hear five short conversations.
You will hear each conversation twice.
There is one question for each conversation.
For each question, choose the right answer (A, B or C).

1 What's Holly doing now?

Boy: Holly wasn't at swimming practice today. Is she ill?
Girl: No, she's fine. She's in the mountains with her family.
Boy: Really? Is she mountain biking again?
Girl: No, she's learning to climb. She's got a great teacher.

2 How much is Jenny's new tennis racket?

Boy: I love your new tennis shoes. Were they expensive?
Girl: No, they weren't. They were £35. My racket was more expensive.
Boy: Oh really? How much was that?
Girl: I bought it online for £40. My sister paid £45 for hers.

3 What time does the hockey match start?

Girl: Excuse me. What time does the hockey match start?
Man: It starts at half past four.
Girl: What time is it now? Am I late?
Man: No, it's only ten past four. Go for a walk and come back at twenty past four.

4 What is Simon drinking?

Girl: I'm thirsty after that race.
Simon: This lemonade is really good. I bought it over there in the café.
Girl: Is there any juice?
Simon: I don't think so, but they've got hot chocolate if you prefer that.

5 Who is Maisie's table-tennis coach?

Maisie: That's my table-tennis coach over there.
Boy: Who? Is he that blond man over there with glasses?
Maisie: No, he's got dark hair and he doesn't wear glasses.
Boy: Oh, I can see him now. He's standing over there next to Brendan.

Unit 6

Recording script

Listen to Ethan talking to his mum about his family.
How are Ethan's family getting to his birthday party?
For questions 1–5 write a letter A–H next to each person.

Ethan: I'm home! Where are you?
Mum: Hi, Ethan! I'm in the kitchen. Happy Birthday!
Ethan: Thanks mum! But where is everyone else? Why are they so late for my party?
Mum: Well, your sister has football practice until 6.00 p.m. Then she's coming home by bus.
Ethan: Why doesn't she take the tram? It's much faster. And where's Dad?
Mum: He phoned fifteen minutes ago. Your grandma missed the half past five bus so your dad is going to drive her.
Ethan: Is Granddad coming in Dad's car, too?
Mum: He had to work this afternoon so he's going to take the underground. It's probably quicker than the car, anyway.
Ethan: I can hear a motorbike. Is that Uncle Tom?
Mum: I spoke to him this morning. He's going to take a taxi after his meeting.
Ethan: Is Ursula coming with him? Or is she taking the underground?
Mum: Your cousin Ursula's cycling here right now. She'll be here in ten minutes. Don't worry!
Ethan: Great! Who else is coming?
Mum: My sister!
Ethan: Aunt May?
Mum: Yes, she's getting the tram from her house to the train station at the end of our road.
Ethan: Mum! What's that noise in the living room?
Voices: Surprise! Happy Birthday ...

Acknowledgements

Author acknowledgements

The author would like to thank her editors, Anne-Marie Murphy, Sara Bennett, James Frith and Judith Greet, for their support and encouragement.

She would like to dedicate this book to her children, Sara and Alex.

Corpus

Development of this publication has made use of the Cambridge English Corpus (CEC). The CEC is a computer database of contemporary spoken and written English, which currently stands at over one billion words. It includes British English, American English and other varieties of English. It also includes the Cambridge Learner Corpus, developed in collaboration with the University of Cambridge ESOL Examinations. Cambridge University Press has built up the CEC to provide evidence about language use that helps to produce better language teaching materials.

English Profile

This product is informed by the English Vocabulary Profile, built as part of English Profile, a collaborative programme designed to enhance the learning, teaching and assessment of English worldwide. Its main funding partners are Cambridge University Press and Cambridge ESOL and its aim is to create a 'profile' for English linked to the Common European Framework of Reference for Languages (CEF). English Profile outcomes, such as the English Vocabulary Profile, will provide detailed information about the language that learners can be expected to demonstrate at each CEF level, offering a clear benchmark for learners' proficiency. For more information, please visit www.englishprofile.org

Illustrations by:

John Batten (Beehive Illustration) pp. 17, 29, 37, 53; Kate Rochester (Pickled Ink) pp. 21; Richard Jones (Beehive Illustration) pp. 45